ALEXANDER BRENNER
A HOLISTIC ART OF BUILDING

 PARK BOOKS   **VILLAS AND HOUSES 2015–2022   VOLUME 3**

sammlungen, gewerbliche, städtebauliche und innenarchitektonische Projekte geplant.

Als Hochschullehrer unterrichtete er in verschiedenen Fachbereichen, so von 1988 bis 2008 Räumliches Gestalten und von 1990 bis 2006 Städtebau an der Hochschule Stuttgart und zuletzt als Gastprofessor für Entwerfen an der Hochschule Biberach.

Viele seiner Arbeiten wurden von der Architektenkammer und dem Bund Deutscher Architektinnen und Architekten (BDA) ausgezeichnet. Das Haus am Oberen Berg wurde für den Europäischen Architekturpreis Mies van der Rohe Award 2009 nominiert.

Die Arbeiten Alexander Brenners genießen seit Langem höchste internationale Anerkennung und wurden weltweit zahlreich in Zeitschriften und Büchern publiziert.

Die Berufung in den BDA erfolgte 1994 und die in den Konvent der Bundesstiftung Baukultur im Jahr 2009/12.

Seit 2020 leiten die assoziierten Partner Benjamin Callies und Markus Sauter zusammen mit ihm das ca. 20-köpfige Team im Atelier im Stuttgarter Norden.

2011, 2013 und 2015 erschienen umfassende Werkmonographien über seine skulpturalen, ganzheitlichen Arbeiten. Zahlreiche Einzelausstellungen in Hamburg, München, Berlin und Stuttgart fanden vor allem im Zusammenhang mit dem Erscheinen der Monographien statt.

Alexander Brenner HOUSES Vol. 1, 1990–2010

Alexander Brenner VILLAS AND HOUSES Vol. 2, 2010–15

Das Goethe Institut Deutschland zählt Alexander Brenner seit 2016 zu den Top Ten Architekten Deutschlands.

and interior design projects.

As a university lecturer, he taught in various fields, including spatial design from 1988 to 2008 and urban design from 1990 to 2006 at the Hochschule für Technik in Stuttgart. Most recently, he was a visiting professor for design at the Biberach University of Applied Sciences.

Many of his projects have received awards from the Chamber of Architects and the Association of German Architects (BDA). The Haus am Oberen Berg was nominated for the 2009 European Union Prize for Contemporary Architecture – Mies van der Rohe Award.

Alexander Brenner's work has long enjoyed the highest international recognition and has been published in numerous journals and books worldwide.

He was appointed to the BDA in 1994 and to the Convention of the Bundesstiftung Baukultur in 2009/12.

Since 2020, the associated partners Benjamin Callies and Markus Sauter together with Alexander Brenner have been leading the approx. 20-member team in the atelier in the north of Stuttgart.

Comprehensive work monographs on his sculptural, holistic projects were published in 2011, 2013 and 2015. Numerous solo exhibitions in Hamburg, Munich, Berlin and Stuttgart took place mainly in connection with the publication of these monographs.

Alexander Brenner HOUSES Vol. 1, 1990–2010

Alexander Brenner VILLAS AND HOUSES Vol. 2, 2010–15

The Goethe Institut Deutschland has ranked Alexander Brenner among Germany's top ten architects since 2016.

www.alexanderbrenner.de

ALEXANDER BRENNER
A HOLISTIC ART OF BUILDING

VILLAS AND HOUSES 2015–2022 VOLUME 3

Impressum | Imprint

Konzept und Gestaltung | Concept and design: Alexander Brenner, Marc Büchler
Übersetzung | Translation: Bianca Murphy, Hamburg
Lektorat | Copyediting: Katrin Pollems-Braunfels, München, Susanne Moser, Stuttgart
Lithografie | Image processing: Reproline Mediateam, Unterföhring
Druck und Bindung | Printing and binding: Passavia Druckservice, Passau
Herausgeber | Editor: B-and, Alexander Brenner Architects, Stuttgart

© 2023 Park Books AG, Zürich
© Texte und Bilder | Texts and photographs: B-and, Alexander Brenner Architects, Stuttgart

Park Books
Niederdorfstrasse 54
8001 Zürich
Schweiz | Switzerland
www.park-books.com

Park Books wird vom Bundesamt für Kultur mit einem Strukturbeitrag für die Jahre 2021–2024 unterstützt.
Park Books is being supported by the Federal Office of Culture with a general subsidy for the years 2021–2024.

Alle Rechte vorbehalten; kein Teil dieses Werks darf in irgendeiner Form ohne vorherige schriftliche Genehmigung des Verlags reproduziert oder unter Verwendung elektronischer Systeme verarbeitet, vervielfältigt oder verbreitet werden.
All rights reserved; no part of this publication may be reproduced, stored in a retrieval system or transmitted in any form or by any means, electronic, mechanical, photocopying, recording, or otherwise, without the prior written consent of the publisher.

ISBN 978-3-03860-268-2

Content

2015 – 2022   Volume 3

Poems of Stone Alexander Brenner	6
Committed to Beauty Holger Reiners	10
Rudolph House Stuttgart, 2021	18
Fineway House Reutlingen, 2020	72
Brenner Research House Stuttgart, 2019	112
Crown House Frankfurt, 2018	186
Haus am Wald Stuttgart, 2016	238
Rottmann House Wiesbaden, 2016	264
The Longing for the Total Work of Art Alexander Brenner	302
List of Works	316
**Bibliography	Credits**	320

GEDICHTE AUS STEIN

ALEXANDER BRENNER

Über drei Dekaden ringen wir nun um das Gute, Schöne und Wahre.

Da ist es wohl auch an der Zeit, einmal darüber nachzudenken, was entstanden ist und warum es so entstanden ist. Erinnere ich mich an die Anfänge meines Studiums zurück, so war dies eine Zeit, als im Grundstudium an der Universität Stuttgart das Konstruktive im Sinne der klassischen Moderne, genauer von Mies van der Rohe, vertreten durch Peter von Seidlein, ganz im Vordergrund stand. Ich bin dankbar, das Konstruieren dort gelernt zu haben. Es gab mir eine gewisse Sicherheit zu wissen, wie man etwas bauen kann.

Im Hauptstudium brachen dann mit Macht die Ideen der Postmoderne auch an der Hochschule Stuttgart durch, was 1984 mit der neuen Staatsgalerie von James Stirling und Michael Wilford eine wahre Euphorie befeuerte. In den Korrekturen zu den Hochschulentwürfen wurden von den Assistenten dann gerne mal ein Architrav oder eine Säulenhalle hineinskizziert, was bei mir zu einem intensiveren Fernbleiben führte.

Mir erschien das Vorblenden und Aufkleben und das Zitieren baugeschichtlichen Halbwissens nicht als zeitgemäßer Weg für die Architektur, und ich war enttäuscht darüber, dass ausgerechnet in dem Moment, als ich wissbegierig lernen wollte, dieser Zeitunfall, wie ich es damals nannte, geschah.

Ich machte mich auf die Suche. Zum Glück wurden zu dieser Zeit die Häuser von Le Corbusier am Weissenhof von Restauratoren untersucht und wiederhergestellt, und durch meine Besuche dort verstand ich, dass die frühe klassische Moderne wenig mit ihrer Interpretation in den Fünfziger- bis Achtzigerjahren zu tun hatte. Als Hoffnungsschimmer erschien mir die Tessiner Schule, insbesondere bewunderte ich die einfache Schönheit der Bauten von Luigi Snozzi. Auf vielen Reisen studierte ich die Werke von Lois Welzenbacher, Guiseppe Terragni, Rudolf Olgiati und Carlo Scarpa. Aber auch aus Vorarlberg kamen frische Ideen, und zu Lesen fand ich viel von Aldo Rossi bis Rem Koolhaas. Es gab also doch einen großen, bunten Strauß spannender Theorien, Architekturen und eine große Zahl an Möglichkeiten.

Der etwas beengten Sicht der frühen Jahre entfloh ich an der Hochschule durch meinen neu gewählten Schwerpunkt Städtebau, der damals von Klaus Humpert gelehrt wurde. Dessen positive, erfrischende Art und herrliche Offenheit gab mir die Möglichkeit, frei zu arbeiten.

Architektur studierte ich für mich selbst, und das Machen erlernte ich im studienbegleitenden intensiven Arbeiten. Die Herausforderung war, nicht aktuelle Tenden-

POEMS OF STONE

ALEXANDER BRENNER

For more than three decades now, we have been struggling for the good, the beautiful and the genuine. It is probably time to reflect on what has been created and why it has been created this way.

Looking back at the early days of my studies, it was a time when the constructive in the sense of classical modernism, more precisely of Mies van der Rohe, represented by Peter von Seidlein, was very much in the foreground in the basic studies at the University of Stuttgart. I am grateful to have learned how to construct at this university, and it gave me a certain security to know how to build something.

In my main studies, the ideas of post-modernism began to vehemently break through at the University of Stuttgart, with the new State Gallery by James Stirling and Michael Wilford fuelling a veritable euphoria in 1984. At the university, the assistants would often correct the concepts we had to present by sketching in an architrave or a portico, which led to intensive absenteeism on my part.

To me, facing and pasting on and quoting superficial knowledge of building history did not seem to be a contemporary way of doing architecture, and I was disappointed that, just when I was eager for knowledge, this accident of time, as I called it at the time, happened.

Therefore, I started searching. Fortunately, at that time, Le Corbusier's houses at the Weissenhof estate were being studied and then reconstructed by restorers, and through my visits there I understood that early classical modernism had little to do with its interpretation in the nineteen-fifties to eighties. The Ticino School seemed to me to be a glimmer of hope and, in particular, I admired the simple beauty of Luigi Snozzi's buildings. On many trips I studied the works of Lois Welzenbacher, Guiseppe Terragni, Rudolf Olgiati and Carlo Scarpa, but fresh ideas also came from the Vorarlberg region, and there was a lot to read from Aldo Rossi to Rem Koolhaas. So, there was a large, colourful bunch of exciting theories, architectures and a large number of possibilities after all.

I escaped the somewhat cramped view of the early years at the university through my newly chosen specialisation in urban planning, which was then taught by Klaus Humpert and whose positive, refreshing manner and wonderful openness gave me the opportunity to work freely.

I studied architecture on my own, and I learned how to actively do it by working intensively while studying. The challenge was not to follow current trends or even fash-

zen oder gar Moden zu verfolgen, sondern eine Haltung zu entwickeln, die als Ausdruck ihrer Zeit auch persönliche Erkenntnisse und sinnliche Erfahrungen mit Gebautem zu einer Gewissheit vereint.

Ich glaube heute noch, dass es nicht möglich ist, jeden Tag alles neu zu erfinden. Aber es liegt in der Verantwortung des Architekten, mit Leidenschaft und Hingabe Räume für Menschen zu erdenken und sie dann mit Liebe zum Detail zu realisieren, denn das Detail, das Material und das mit größter Sorgfalt Geschaffene ist das, was Menschen wahrhaftig berührt. Architektur ist eine der ganz wenigen Möglichkeiten, Liebe und Hingabe so zu konservieren, dass sie auch von späteren Generationen noch gelesen und erfahren werden kann. Jeder hat schon einmal die Erfahrung gemacht, meist bei Altbauten, dass der sorgfältig ausgearbeitete Raum die Fähigkeit besitzt, in uns Stimmungen und eine scheinbar unbegründete Heiterkeit zu erzeugen, oft als Gefühl des Geborgenseins oder zumindest als einer bereichernden Übereinstimmung.

Deshalb verfolgen wir seit Beginn unserer Arbeit das Ziel, mit schönen Räumen den Menschen Freude zu bereiten, beim ersten Betreten, aber auch für die lange Zeit danach. Der Innenraum ist das, was den Menschen direkt umgibt, den er täglich nutzt.

Dabei ist es die dauerhaft und solide gemachte Handarbeit, die ihm aufgrund der Funktion, aber auch der Form ans Herz wächst. Oft werden wir gefragt, ob es denn nicht zu viel Mühe mache, für jedes Haus alles neu zu zeichnen und zu detaillieren. Aber genau darin sehen wir unsere Aufgabe und Pflicht. Wir halten es für das Nachhaltigste überhaupt, ein Haus als Ganzes, mit seinen Einrichtungsgegenständen und Möbeln so zu konstruieren und zu gestalten, dass es schön anzuschauen ist, sehr, sehr lange gebraucht werden kann und nicht wie billig gemachte und modisch gestaltete Industrieprodukte nach kurzer Zeit ersetzt werden muss.

Das Bedürfnis nach dem Echten, nach dem Wahren, das man tasten und erfahren kann, ist heute größer denn je, gerade in einer Zeit, die zunehmend bildhafter und virtueller wird. Ein Haus und eine Wohnung sind keine Illusion, sondern ein persönliches, nicht vom Architekten zu bestimmendes, sondern künstlerisch übersetztes Lebensmodell, das den Bewohnern ein Leben mit Sinnlichkeit, Musik, Kunst, Geist und Phantasie schenkt. Dem Menschen dies zu geben und sein Bedürfnis nach Schönheit zu stillen, heißt, all die Aufschwünge seiner Seele zu respektieren und die Kunst des Lebens zuzulassen.

ions but to develop an attitude that, on the one hand, is an expression of its time, but on the other hand, also unites personal insights and sensual experiences with built structures into a certainty.

Today, I still believe that it`s not possible to reinvent everything every day, but that it is the architect's responsibility to conceive spaces for people with passion and dedication and then to implement them with attention to detail. Since the detail, the material and everything that is created with utmost care is what touches people in the truest sense. Architecture is one of the few ways to preserve love and devotion so that it can still be understood and experienced by later generations. Everyone has made the experience, usually in old buildings, that the carefully crafted space has the ability to create moods and a seemingly unfounded serenity in us, often as a sense of security, or at least an enriching correspondence.

That is why, from the very beginning, we have pursued the vision of creating beautiful rooms that give people pleasure when they first enter them, but also for a long time afterwards. The interior is what directly surrounds people, the space they use every day, and here it is the durable and solidly handcrafted work that grows dear to their hearts because of its function, but also because of its form. We are often asked if it is not too much effort to draw and elaborate everything down to the last detail for every house, but this is exactly what we see as our task and duty. We consider it the most sustainable thing of all to construct and design the house as a whole, with its fixtures and furnishings, in such a way that it is beautiful to look at and can be used for a very, very long time, instead of having to be replaced after a short time like cheaply made and trendy industrial products.

The need for the genuine, for the true, for what you can touch and experience is greater today than ever before, especially in an age that is becoming increasingly image-based and virtual. The house and the flat are not an illusion but a personal model of life, not to be determined by the architect but artistically translated, thus gives the inhabitants a life with sensuality, music, art, will, spirit and imagination. Giving this to people and satisfying their need for beauty means respecting all the stirrings of their soul and admitting the art of living.

We have always been lucky to find clients, I can see that now in retrospect, who granted us the opportunity to newly develop and rethink the tasks with them and who were very grateful at the end of the process to have been

Rückblickend sehe ich es als großes Glück, dass wir immer Bauherrschaften gefunden haben, die es uns ermöglichten, mit ihnen die anstehenden Aufgaben jeweils neu zu entwickeln und zu denken, und die am Ende des Prozesses sehr dankbar waren, dass sie mehr bekommen haben, als ursprünglich gedacht und gewünscht. Ich bin unendlich froh, dass wir nahezu alles, an dem wir intensiv gearbeitet haben, auch bauen durften. Ich weiß von vielen Kollegen, dass dies nicht selbstverständlich ist. Vielleicht haben wir uns auch nur mit Bauherrschaften verbündet, die, wie wir, emotional mit der Aufgabe verbunden sind und unsere Arbeitsweise, die keine einfachen und bequemen Kompromisse kennt, verstehen und schätzen und gemeisterte Schwierigkeiten als Teil eines besonderen Resultats erachten. Und so spüre ich auch bei jedem Besuch eines unserer Häuser die Begeisterung, die Arbeit und die Leidenschaft, die es damals hervorgebracht hat.

Die Konzentration auf vergleichsweise wenige Projekte und das Arbeiten in einem kleinen, hochmotivierten Team hat sich als Glücksfall erwiesen, ebenso wie die lange Zusammenarbeit mit den Besten ihres Faches.

Alle genannten Randbedingungen kommen im Bautypus des privaten Wohnhauses zusammen, von dem wir hier sechs Projekte ausführlich zeigen möchten.

Auch wenn die Abbildungen nicht den räumlichen Eindruck und die Atmosphäre zu 100 Prozent vermitteln können, so danken wir Zooey Braun, der für uns seit über 15 Jahren unsere Projekte fotografisch dokumentiert, für seine fantastische Arbeit. Einige Aufnahmen, vor allem von Details, hat aber auch die „B-and" beigetragen, also das Atelierteam, dem mein großer Dank für die Mitwirkung bei unseren Fotoshootings gilt, aber vor allem für die großartige tägliche Arbeit an den Projekten. Sie alle haben viel und harte Arbeit geleistet und Außergewöhnliches geschaffen, angeleitet durch meine Partner Benjamin Callies und Markus Sauter, die beide seit ihrem Studium das büroeigene Denken mit überwältigendem Engagement und Begeisterung prägen. Wie durch ein Wunder halten diese Beiden alles im Gleichgewicht, halten den Winden und Stürmen stand und geben aus innerer Überzeugung alles hinein, was es braucht, um Gedichte aus der Erde emporwachsen zu sehen. Ihnen gilt mein besonderer Dank. Alles, was wir erschaffen durften, verdanken wir unseren Bauherren, den Handwerkern und Ausführenden und einer großen Zahl von Menschen, die mit uns gearbeitet haben. Ihnen allen danke ich von Herzen und hoffe auf ihre weitere Unterstützung beim Erschaffen von Bauwerken, die Ausdruck architektonischer Verantwortung sind und ein Abbild von Liebe und Lebensfreude.

given more than they had originally imagined or asked for. I am immensely happy that we had the chance to build almost everything we worked on intensively; and I know from many colleagues that this is not a matter of course. Perhaps we have only teamed up with clients who, like us, are emotionally connected to the task and understand and appreciate our way of working, which knows no easy and convenient compromises, and consider mastered difficulties as part of a special result. So, every time I visit one of our houses, I feel the enthusiasm, the work and the passion that produced it at the time.

Concentrating on a comparatively small number of projects and working in a small, highly motivated team has proven to be a stroke of luck, as has the long collaboration with the best in their profession.

Yet all of the above-mentioned boundary conditions usually cumulate in the building type of the private residence, of which we would like to present six projects in detail in this book.

Even though the images cannot fully convey the spatial impression and atmosphere, we thank Zooey Braun, who has been photographically documenting our projects for us for over 15 years, for his fantastic work. Some shots, especially of details, have been contributed by the "B-and", our studio team, who deserve my sincere thanks for their participation in our photo shoots, but above all for their great day-to-day work on the projects. They all have put in a lot of hard work and achieved extraordinary results, guided by my partners Benjamin Callies and Markus Sauter, both of whom have been shaping the studio's philosophy with overwhelming commitment and enthusiasm since their studies. Miraculously, the two of them keep everything in balance, withstand the winds and storms and, out of inner conviction, put in everything it takes to see poems emerge from the ground. They deserve my special thanks. Everything we had the privilege to create we owe to our clients, the craftsmen and those who executed the work, and a large number of people who have worked with us. I thank them all from the bottom of my heart and hope for their continued support in creating buildings that are an expression of architectural responsibility and a reflection of love and joy of life.

AM OBEREN BERG, 2007, from the book ALEXANDER BRENNER - HOUSES 1990-2010 Vol. 1

COMMITTED TO BEAUTY
ATTEMPT AT AN APPRECIATION

HOLGER REINERS

In recent years, there have been endless publications on Alexander Brenner's architectural work: numerous monographs, an innumerable number of articles in both national and international journals, in many languages and translations – always with the same tenor: Alexander Brenner is one of the big names in contemporary architecture. Is there any substantial aspect that I can add to this appreciation in unison that has not been considered so far? I will try.

In the past 100 years or so, there have been few formulations of epochal significance that have captivated the architectural world, mostly unchallenged, to this day. These quotations are familiar to every architecture student even before the first semester, and they continue to have their full effect to this day – ex cathedra, as it were –, doubts are neither desired nor permitted. Of course, I am not entering uncharted intellectual territory with my thoughts outlined here. In short: everything has been there before. Or perhaps it hasn't?

Austrian architect Adolf Loos gave his momentous lecture entitled "Ornament and Crime" in Vienna in 1908. The text of his speech was subsequently published in all cultural languages of the world. Adolf Loos stated: "I have discovered the following truth and present it to the world: cultural evolution is equivalent to the removal of ornament from articles in daily use." Elsewhere he said: "The lack of ornament means shorter working hours and consequently higher wages. Ornament is wasted labour." And: "Lack of ornament is a sign of spiritual strength." This scathingly polemic still has an impact today. It is the final reckoning with historicism and its exuberant adornment of the most diverse façade styles. I will come back to that later.

The equally pugnacious, momentous and polarising quotation in the history of architecture is "form follows function" and is usually only quoted in abbreviated form – originally it read "form ever follows function". American architect Louis Sullivan, who was just 30 years old at the time, applied the concept to architecture in Chicago in 1896. Unlike for Loos, the decoration of a façade – also – had a very special function for him: that of a comprehensible visual language and message, as the Prudential Building completed in 1896 in Buffalo, New York, impressively shows. Sullivan speaks of the emotional nature of buildings.

The synthesis of these two influential demands on architectural aspirations was later described by Frank Lloyd Wright with these words: "Form follows function – that has been misunderstood. Form and function should be

Eine Synthese dieser zwei einflussreichen Ansprüche an die Architektur hat Frank Lloyd Wright dann später so formuliert: „Form follows function – that has been misunderstood. Form and function should be one, joined in spiritual union." Nicht zufällig war Sullivan dann später der Mentor von Frank Lloyd Wright. Mit dieser erweiterten Interpretation hätte Frank Lloyd Wright, wäre sie denn ebenso einflussreich für die Architekturgeschichte bis heute geworden, besonders in Deutschland ein anderes Architekturgeschehen – für das anspruchsvolle Wohnhaus bewirkt. Vielleicht hätte es sogar bei weniger Widerstand eine ganz neue, innovative Architektursprache gegeben.

Alexander Brenner hat für seine Monografie III den Titel „A Holistic Art of Building" gewählt und damit eine verbindliche Zukunftsforderung für Architekten und Auftraggeber nicht nur in Deutschland formuliert: als ganzheitlich umfassende, planerische Lösung für jede Phase des Entwurfsprozesses im Detail und schließlich gebaut als Summe seiner Teile, als sicht- und deutbare Architektur der Eleganz.

Aber noch einmal zurück zum Anfang. Wo sehe ich Alexander Brenner in der aktuellen Architekturdiskussion? Ich erlebe schon lange eine in weiten Teilen sensibilisierte Öffentlichkeit: Nicht nur innerhalb des Fachs beherrscht feindseliger Meinungsdissens die Diskussion und ein Beharren auf das eigene Entwurfsverständnis, die eigene Architektur. Unversöhnlich stehen sich das Lager der „zeitgenössischen Moderne" auf der einen und die Position der „Fortschreibung einer Entwurfs- und Bautradition" auf der anderen Seite des Spektrums gegenüber, die für sich ebenfalls eine Daseinsberechtigung im Architekturgeschehen beansprucht, auch wenn diese Richtung nur etwa drei Prozent aller Auftragsvolumen ausmacht. Unter diese drei Prozent von Architekten subsumiere ich allerdings nur diejenigen, die ihre Entwurfsarbeit auch als ganzheitlich verstehen und die gekonnt mit den überlieferten Stilvorgaben umgehen können. Ich meine also gerade nicht die „Möchtegern-Klassiker", die ihre trostlosen Hüllen verkaufsfördernd mit einem Säulenvordach, betonten Faschen um die Fenster oder einem Bossenputz versehen, um vertraute baugeschichtliche Stilmerkmale aufzunehmen, die architektonische Kennerschaft vortäuschen. Dass die neuen Vertreter des Bauhauses diese Art von Architekturklitterung als Schande für den Berufsstand ablehnen, ist nur zu verständlich – und ich teile ihre Meinung.

Ganz anders verhält es sich mit den Könnern einer Fortschreibung bewährter stilistischer Bautraditionen im

one, joined in spiritual union." It is no coincidence that Sullivan later became Frank Lloyd Wright's mentor. With this expanded interpretation, had it been just as influential for the history of architecture up to the present day, Frank Lloyd Wright would have, especially in Germany, brought about a different architectural development for the sophisticated residential house, which would have certainly looked different for the last two generations and up to the present day. If confronted with less resistance, there might even have evolved a completely new, innovative architectural vocabulary.

Alexander Brenner has chosen the title "A holistic art of building" for his Monograph III, thereby formulating a binding future demand for both architects and clients, not only in Germany: a holistically comprehensive planning solution for every phase of the design process in every detail and finally built as the sum of its parts, as a visible and interpretable architecture of elegance.

But let's go back to the beginning. Where do I see Alexander Brenner in the current architectural discourse? I have observed a large, sensitised public for some time now: it is not only within the discipline that hostile dissent dominates the discussion and an insistence on one's own understanding of design, one's own architecture. It is the two irreconcilable camps of "contemporary modernism" on the one side and the "continuation of a design and building tradition" on the other side of the spectrum that also claims a raison d'être for itself in the architectural scene, even though it only accounts for about three percent of all commissions. However, among these three percent of architects, I only include those who understand their design work to be holistic and who are adept at dealing with the traditional style guidelines. I am not referring to the "wannabe classicists" who cleverly adorn their bleak shells with a columned canopy, accentuated mouldings around the windows or bossage-like plaster in order to incorporate seemingly familiar architectural style features that feign architectural expertise. It is perfectly understandable that the new representatives of the Bauhaus reject this kind of architectural patchwork as a disgrace to the profession – and I share their view.

The situation is completely different when it comes to the experts in continuing tried and tested stylistic building traditions in the sense of Gottfried Semper: here, architecture is understood as an art of "dressing" buildings in decorative textile-like façades, which has shaped an entire epoch of architectural history: historicism. I defend these neo-historical designs solely because they require a high degree of connoisseurship and expertise – no

Sinne von Gottfried Semper: Hier wird die Architektur als Bekleidungskunst verstanden, die eine ganze Epoche des Architekturgeschehens geprägt hat: den Historismus. Ich verteidige diese neohistoristischen Entwürfe allein deshalb, weil sie ein hohes Maß an Kenner- und Könnerschaft voraussetzen – ohne umfassende baugeschichtliche Kenntnisse ergibt sich kein überzeugendes Erscheinungsbild.

Mein Blick auf die „Moderne" fällt kritisch aus. Die Kunstgeschichte spricht von 1900 an von „Moderne". Wie verträgt sich dieser Begriff mit der heutigen Gegenwartsarchitektur, welcher Qualität auch immer? Jugendstil und Art Déco stehen für die beiden letzten, originären Architekturepochen, die noch den Begriff des „Stils" verkörpern – und danach? Danach werden noch der Expressionismus und die Arts-and-Crafts-Bewegung als Stilepoche erfasst, also die Zeit bis etwa zum Ende der Zwanzigerjahre. Alle anderen architektonischen Zeugnisse fallen unter den Begriff der „Moderne". Das bedeutet nichts anderes, als dass die Ideen des Bauhauses cum grano salis bis in unsere Gegenwart tradiert wurden und bis heute als verbindlich angesehen werden. Man könnte auch kritisch resümieren: Den deutschen Architekten ist seit den Fünfzigerjahren nicht mehr viel Neues eingefallen.

Warum habe ich diesen, zugegeben, langen Vorspann gewählt? Weil den Projekten von Alexander Brenner eine ganz besondere Bedeutung im Baugeschehen zukommt. Das belegen unter anderem die Vorgängerpublikationen I und II, die für einen Paradigmenwechsel stehen: Hier tritt jemand selbstbewusst unseren zeittypischen Erwartungen entgegen, was denn Architektur ausmachen und leisten soll. Hier wird die Botschaft einer sinnlich erfahrbaren, emotional geprägten Architektur auf höchstem Niveau vertreten, einer holistisch verstandenen Architektur, die sehr viel mehr erwarten lässt als die Erfüllung des längst abgenutzten Begriffs der Ganzheitlichkeit.

Das ist ein neues, ein breites Selbstverständnis, das die Öffentlichkeit schon lange einfordert. Eine Architektur der Schönheit, die ihre Verantwortung einlöst. Es sind gebaute Lösungen, die sich aus der gegenwärtigen Architektur von Alexander Brenner auch auf jeden anderen Größenmaßstab übertragen ließen.

In welchem Verhältnis zu den beiden oben genannten Polen steht die Architektur von Alexander Brenner? Sein Werk grenzt sich deutlich ab, es ist keinem der beiden Lager zuzuordnen, aber man tut ihm sicher nicht Unrecht, wenn man behauptet, dass er sich dem unbedingten Ge-

convincing appearance emerges without all-embracing knowledge of building history.

My take on "modernism" is a critical one. Art history speaks of "modernism" from 1900 onwards. How is this term compatible with today's contemporary architecture, regardless of its quality? Art Nouveau and Art Déco stand for the last two genuine architectural epochs that still embody the concept of "style" – and after that? Expressionism and the Arts and Crafts movement are still considered as stylistic eras, i.e. the period up to the end of the 1920s. All other architectural testimonies come under the heading of "modernism". What that means is that the ideas of the Bauhaus have been handed down cum grano salis to our present day and continue to be regarded as mandatory. Another critical summary could be: German architects have not come up with a great deal of new ideas since the 1950s.

Why have I chosen this, admittedly lengthy, preface? Because Alexander Brenner's projects have a very special significance in the building field. This is evidenced, among other things, by the previous publications I and II, which represent a paradigm shift: here is someone who self-confidently confronts our typical expectations as to what constitutes architecture and what it is supposed to achieve. Here, the message of an architecture that can be experienced by the senses, that is shaped by emotions, is represented at the highest level, an architecture that is understood to be holistic and that gives us reason to expect much more than the fulfilment of the long since hackneyed concept of holism.

This is a new, a broad self-conception that the public has been demanding for a long time. An architecture of beauty that lives up to its responsibility. The projects are built solutions that could be transferred from Alexander Brenner's current architecture to any other scale.

What is the relationship between Alexander Brenner's architecture and the two poles mentioned above? His oeuvre clearly demarcates itself, it cannot be assigned to either camp, but it is certainly not doing Brenner injustice to claim that he feels committed to the unconditional will to design of the Bauhaus doctrine of the early years – yet without any dogmatism. Alexander Brenner creates a very unique architecture that defies any preconceived image of a "villa today". Anyone who delves into the design concepts of his buildings will discover that, for him, architecture implies its expansion into art in every project – in other words, elevating architecture to another dimension, the spiritual and almost magical. This conceptual dimension can be experienced in all of his pro-

staltungswillen der Bauhaus-Lehre der Anfangsjahre verpflichtet fühlt – allerdings ohne jeden Dogmatismus. Alexander Brenner schafft eine ganz eigene Architektur, die sich dem vorgefassten Bild einer „Villa heute" entzieht. Wer sich einmal in die Entwurfskonzepte seiner Bauten vertieft, wird feststellen, dass für ihn die Architektur bei jedem Projekt ihre Erweiterung in die Kunst impliziert – also Baukunst in eine andere Dimension erhöht, ins Geistige und beinahe Magische. Diese entwurfliche Dimension ist in allen seinen Gebäuden erfahrbar. Es ist genau das, was eine „große Hand" im Architekturgeschehen ausmacht, die selbstbewusste und sichere Hand eines freien Geistes.

Es ist erst zwei Generationen her, dass jede Form von „Geniekult" an den Hochschulen verpönt war. Extravaganzen wurden weder erwartet, noch waren sie im Curriculum des Architekturstudiums vorgesehen. Trauten wir angehenden Architekten zu wenig zu, oder sollten sie sich nur in einem bestimmten, also genehmigten, gestalterischen Rahmen bewegen? Natürlich hat sich daran bis heute vieles geändert, doch bei der Präsentation von Diplomarbeiten ebenso wie bei den Ausstellungen zu großen Wettbewerben dominiert heute der Einfluss von sachlichen, an Formen armen Entwürfen. Daran ändern auch die so genannten „markanten" Entwürfe in Hamburg, der „Elbtower" oder die „tanzenden Türme" nichts, außer dass sie eine ungewohnte Größe oder eine effekthaschende Form darbieten.

Auch wenn die Dimensionen im Werk von Alexander Brenner andere sind, also nicht durch schiere Größe auf sich aufmerksam machen, so sind sie in meiner Wertschätzung gerade deshalb von besonderer Bedeutung. Darauf komme ich in der Betrachtung der in diesem Band vorgestellten Bauten von Alexander Brenner zurück, immer unter dem Aspekt, worin zeigt sich hier das Einzigartige, also das, was sich nicht über die Architektur eines anderen Architekten übertragen lässt – es sei denn als ärmlich-verkrampfte Kopie, von denen inzwischen zu viele entstanden sind. Wobei man in beinahe jedem Neubaugebiet Versuche findet, zumindest Versatzstücke Brenner'scher Architektur aufzugreifen.

Ich messe die Kraft und die partielle Einzigartigkeit im Villenbau an den Großen, die mir spontan einfallen. Das sind für das 19. und die Zwanzigerjahre des 20. Jahrhunderts beispielhaft Otto Wagner und Josef Hoffmann, die genialen Entwürfe von Victor Horta und Frank Lloyd Wright sowie Josep Levis Sert in Frankreich, bei den Traditionalisten ist es Mott B. Schmidt in New York. Die Projekte dieser Großen – das ist meine Auswahl, ande-

jects. It is precisely what constitutes a "great hand" in the architectural field, the self-confident and sure hand of a free spirit.

Only two generations ago, any form of "genius cult" was frowned upon at universities. Extravaganzas were neither expected nor provided for in the curriculum of architectural studies. Did we not have enough confidence in the architects-to-be, or were they only supposed to move within a certain, i.e. approved, creative framework? Of course, a lot has already changed in this respect by now, but the current presentation of diploma theses or the exhibitions accompanying major competitions are dominated by the influence of factual designs that are poor in form. Even the so-called "striking" designs in Hamburg, the Elbtower or the Dancing Towers, do not change this, except that they boast an unusual size or a gimmicky shape.

Even though the scale of Alexander Brenner's work is different, i.e. does not draw attention to itself through sheer size, it is for precisely this reason that it is of particular importance in my appreciation. I will come back to this in my consideration of Alexander Brenner's projects presented in this volume, always under the aspect of what is it that reflects the unique, in other words, what cannot be transferred to someone else's architecture – except as a poor, stilted copy, of which too many have meanwhile been built. Even though one finds attempts in almost every newly developed residential estate to adopt at least set pieces of Brenner's architecture.

I compare the power and partial uniqueness in villa construction with the great names that come to my mind spontaneously. For the 19th century and the 1920s, Otto Wagner and Josef Hoffmann are examples, as are Victor Horta and Frank Lloyd Wright with their ingenious designs, and Josep Levis Sert in France; for the traditionalists it is Mott B. Schmidt in New York. The projects of these masters – that's my selection; others certainly have their own names – they all have in common is the immediate impression of unique creative talent, even genius, in every facet of their designs. This spiritual aspect of a design is difficult to put into words, it is an encoding of expression and a subjective artistic summary. My assessment can be verified in all facets of Alexander Brenner's architecture by the projects presented in this Volume III.

Genius in the context of architecture is of course a big word, so I like to name the criteria that are important to me in this regard: originality of the building in the site

re haben sicher ihre eigenen Namen – verbindet der in jeder Facette ihrer Entwürfe unmittelbare Eindruck der einzigartigen schöpferischen Veranlagung, ja Genialität. Dieses Geistige eines Entwurfs lässt sich schwer in Worte fassen, es ist eine Verschlüsselung des Ausdrucks und eine subjektive künstlerische Zusammenfassung. Überprüfen lässt sich meine Einschätzung in allen Facetten der Architektur von Alexander Brenner an den hier im Volume III vorgestellten Projekten.

Genialität im Zusammenhang mit Architektur ist natürlich ein großes Wort, darum nenne ich gern die Kriterien, die für mich in diesem Zusammenhang wichtig sind: Originalität des Baukörpers im Kontext des Grundstücks, die grafische Plastizität der Fassade, ihr Relief oder ihre skulpturale Form, und der Zusammenklang der Materialien. Jedes einzelne ist nicht austauschbar, sondern elementar im Sinne einer ganzheitlichen „sprachlichen Wirkung" und Dramaturgie. Der Fotograf Zooey Braun hat diese Zusammenhänge von Körper, Form, Fläche und Raum mit großem Einfühlungsvermögen dokumentiert. Die genannten Kriterien für eine geniale Architektur setzen sich dabei harmonisch von der Schwelle zwischen Außen- und Innenraum selbstverständlich bis ins Innere des Hauses fort.
Hier sollte sich der Betrachter fragen, ob ihm irgendein Detail im Großen wie im Kleinen auffällt, das zu einer Korrektur einlädt, sowohl in der Form als auch im Material. Wohl kaum. Der Künstlerarchitekt nutzte die Möglichkeiten, die ihm in Entwurf, Ausführung und mit den verschiedenen Materialien zur Verfügung standen, zum Zusammenklingen aller Einzelteile unter dem Anspruch der Perfektion. Die Wirkung jeder einzelnen architektonischen Geste überrascht in der Fokussierung: in der dominanten Großform ebenso wie in jedem Bauteil und den faszinierenden künstlerischen Details.
Alexander Brenner verfolgt mit seinem holistischen Anspruch an das Entwerfen und das Bauen ein Rückbesinnen auf die Sinnlichkeit, die seine originäre Architektur ausmacht: Seine Entwürfe lassen sich ohne die tradierte Kunst des Handwerks nicht realisieren, jedes Bauteil strahlt diese erfahrbare Würde aus. Nichts darf diese Würde beschädigen. Deshalb verzichtet Alexander Brenner beispielhaft auf jedweden Einsatz von industriell hergestellten Massenprodukten aus Kunststoff, die von keinem selbstbewussten Handwerker bearbeitet wurden. Jeder in seinen Projekten verbaute Werkstoff lässt sich darauf überprüfen, ob er „Wärme" oder „Kälte" ausstrahlt. Mit Wärme meine ich die emotionale Natur der

context; the sculptural quality of the façade, its relief or its sculptural form; and the interplay of the materials. None of them is interchangeable, but each one is elementary in the sense of a holistic "linguistic effect" and dramaturgy. The photographer Zooey Braun has documented these interrelationships of volume, form, surface and space with great sensitivity. The aforementioned criteria for ingenious architecture continue harmoniously from the threshold between outside and inside to the interior of the house in a self-evident manner. Here, the viewer should ask himself whether he notices any detail, large or small, that beckons correction, both in form and in material. Probably not. The artist-architect exploited all the possibilities that were available to him during the design, the execution and in the complex materiality to achieve the consonance of all the individual parts under the claim of perfection. The effect of each individual architectural gesture surprises when brought into focus: both in the dominant large-scale form and in each component and the fascinating artistic details.
With his holistic approach to design and building, Alexander Brenner pursues a return to the sensuality that constitutes his genuine architecture: his designs cannot be implemented without the traditional art of craftsmanship, each component radiates a tangible dignity. Nothing may damage this dignity. Accordingly, Alexander Brenner refrains in an exemplary manner from any use of industrially mass-produced plastic products that have never been worked by a true, self-confident craftsman. Every material used in his projects can be tested to see whether it radiates "warmth" or "cold". By warmth I mean the emotional nature of the visible and the tactile appeal of all the surfaces and structures of his buildings – both in the external shell and in the materials that can be experienced up close, which give each room its "melodically harmonious" effect, its unmistakable aura. Both outside and inside, no effect is left to chance or lack of concentration; each planning step is preceded by numerous sketches, in order to eventually offer, after precise reviews, the harmony that his architecture stands for: a sensual experience. Upon completion, the outcome presents itself in all its beauty – as an artwork of timelessness.

The keyword that permeates all levels of Brenner's designs is the postulate of beauty. Nothing must disturb this unity of monolithic form and sculptural structure. The building as an artefact finds its equivalent in the consummate modelling of the respective contrapuntal

sichtbaren und den haptischen Reiz aller Flächen und Körper seiner Bauwerke – in der äußeren Hülle ebenso wie in den ganz nah erlebbaren Materialien, die jedem Raum seine „melodisch harmonische" Wirkung, seine unverwechselbare Aura verleihen. Außen wie innen, nichts ist in der Wirkung dem Zufall oder einer Unkonzentriertheit überlassen, jedem Planungsschritt gehen zahlreiche Skizzen voraus, um am Ende nach genauen Überprüfungen den Zusammenklang zu bieten, für den seine Architektur steht: ein sinnliches Erleben. Nach der Fertigstellung stellt sich das Ergebnis in seiner ganzen Schönheit dar – als Kunstwerk der Zeitlosigkeit.

Das Stichwort, das alle Ebenen der Entwürfe Brenners durchzieht, ist das Postulat der Schönheit. Nichts darf diese Einheit aus monolithischer Form und plastischer Struktur stören. Das Bauwerk als Artefakt findet seine Entsprechung im vollendeten Modellieren der jeweils kontrapunktischen Gartengestaltung, beides sollte sich im Idealfall zu einem „Gesamtkunstwerk" – ergänzen. An jedem der Projekte dieses Bandes lässt sich dies nachweisen und genießen. Alexander Brenner geht es in der Wirkung stets um das Zusammenklingen von Verhältnissen – also um die Wirkung von Formen, Flächen, Kuben und Raum und der ihnen zugeordneten Kontraste, die dann den großen Spannungsbogen aller Architekturelemente schaffen. Es lohnt sich, diesem Gedanken einmal beim Betrachten der einzelnen Projekte nachzugehen.

Das fertige Bauwerk als Kunstwerk ist die entscheidende Herausforderung für den Architekten Brenner, und dieser Anspruch wird mit derselben Verpflichtung im Raumgefüge, wie in der Wirkung aller Raumschichten zueinander eingelöst. Es geht nie nur um die eindimensionale Fläche, sondern um das Ausloten ihrer ikonografischen Möglichkeiten, um eine offene Wahrnehmung durch den Betrachter – in jedem Fall ein animierender Gewinn.

Es ist kein nachgeordnetes Anliegen, das alle Bauten des Architekten so besonders macht: sein Anspruch an handwerkliche Präzision. Jedes Handwerk hatte einst ein besonderes Verständnis von der Würde des eigenen Tuns. Das ist inzwischen weitgehend verloren gegangen. Alexander Brenner aber steht zu dieser Tradition, „seine" Handwerker wissen um diese Wertschätzung und geben stets ihr Bestes. Architekt und Handwerker wissen um ihre jeweilige Verantwortung und sind sich im gegenseitigen Qualitätsverständnis einig, für beide Seiten auch emotional ein großer Gewinn. Wer wünschte sich am Bau nicht genau das: Den Umgang miteinander

garden design, and both should ideally complement each other to form a "synthesis of the arts". This can be demonstrated and enjoyed with each of the projects featured in this volume. Alexander Brenner is always concerned with the consonance of relations – that is, the effect of forms, surfaces, cubes and space and the corresponding contrasting counterparts, which then create the great arc of suspense of all architectural elements working together. It is worthwhile to remember this idea when looking at the individual projects.

The finished building as a work of art is a decisive challenge for Brenner as an architect, and this aspiration is always redeemed with the same commitment in the spatial structure just as in the effect of all spatial layers in relation to each other. So, it is never a question of the one-dimensionality of a surface, but of exploring its iconographic possibilities, of the viewer's open perception – and in any case an animating benefit.

It is not a subordinate concern that makes all the architect's buildings so special: it is his demand on precision craftsmanship. Each craft once had a special understanding of the dignity of its own practice. This has been largely lost by now. Alexander Brenner, however, stands by this tradition, "his" craftsmen know about this appreciation and always put their best foot forward. Architect and craftsman are aware of their respective responsibilities and agree on their mutual understanding of quality. This is a great benefit for both sides, also emotionally. Mutual respect in dealing with each other: who wouldn't want exactly that on a building site? So, it is also the social competence of the architect that matters, not only in his interaction with the client, but with the same emphasis also in the working relationship with the craftsmen.

Alexander Brenner is an artist-architect. What is behind the aura of this term has unfortunately received too little attention in general perception. Other parameters, such as "holistic building", often are aspiration enough. Of secondary importance are the visible signs of "energy-efficient architecture", assembled from dubious industrial products.

Alexander Brenner demonstrates that there are much better solutions to a building's energy efficiency, for example, the dimension of exterior walls, which do not require any further energy-related measures. Energy efficiency is engineering knowledge that comes naturally to him, yet is never formally obtrusive but artfully concealed as a functional, serving element.

Artist-architect? For his clients, he creates perfectly functioning homes that also live up to this demand in all

in gegenseitigem Respekt. Es geht also auch um die soziale Kompetenz des Architekten, nicht allein im Zusammenspiel zwischen Auftraggeber und Architekt, sondern bei derselben Gewichtung auch um das Verhältnis gegenüber dem „Hand"-Werk.

Alexander Brenner ist ein Künstlerarchitekt. Was sich hinter der Aura dieses Begriffes verbirgt, hat in der allgemeinen Wahrnehmung leider zu wenig Beachtung erfahren. Andere Parameter, wie das „ganzheitliche Bauen", sind oft Anspruch genug. Nachrangig geht es dann um die sichtbaren Zeichen einer „energieeffizienten Architektur", gefügt aus zweifelhaften Industrieprodukten. Alexander Brenner zeigt, dass es viel bessere Lösungen für das Thema Energieeffizienz eines Gebäudes geben kann, wie beispielsweise die Dimensionierung der Außenwände, die keiner weiteren energetischen Maßnahme bedürfen. Energieeffizienz ist ihm selbstverständliches Ingenieurwissen, aber nie formal aufdringlich, sondern kunstvoll verborgen als funktional dienendes Element.

Künstlerarchitekt? Für seine Auftraggeber schafft er perfekt funktionierende Lebensräume, die diesem Anspruch in allen täglichen Aspekten gerecht werden. Bei den Bauten von Alexander Brenner zählt in der Gewichtung kein Aspekt mehr als die anderen, alle sind gleichwertig und bilden ein facettenreiches Zusammenspiel – die alltägliche Funktionalität ebenso wie die Wirkung als erlebbares Kunstwerk. Er zeigt dabei immer wieder, was für ihn ein unverzichtbares Momentum seiner Arbeit ist: vollendete Schönheit. Jedes seiner Projekte steht für seine große Leidenschaft im Umgang mit Architektur und einer unbedingten Verpflichtung seinen Auftraggebern gegenüber, ein beständiges Unikat höchster Qualität zu liefern, ein holistisches Bauwerk im Dienste der Schönheit.

aspects of day-to-day life. In Alexander Brenner's buildings, no one aspect is more important than the others, they are equally weighted and form a multi-faceted interplay – everyday functionality just as much as the impression as a tangible work of art. In doing so, he repeatedly demonstrates what he considers to be an indispensable momentum of his work: consummate beauty. Each of his projects stands for a great passion in dealing with architecture and an unconditional commitment to his clients to deliver a lasting unicum of the highest quality, a holistic building at the service of beauty.

AN DER ACHALM, 2014, from the book ALEXANDER BRENNER - VILLAS AND HOUSES 2010-2015 Vol. 2

RUDOLPH HOUSE
HOME FOR A CAR ENTHUSIAST, STUTTGART
2021

Das Haus für einen Porsche-Enthusiasten und Autosammler steht an einem steilen Hang mit Blick auf die Stadt Stuttgart.
Es liegt, wie das bisherige Haus aus dem Jahr 1998, welches sich direkt daneben befindet, unterhalb einer für Stuttgart typischen Panoramastraße.

Der Weg zum Haus führt zunächst parallel zum Hang. Von hier weitet sich der Blick über das Haus zum ganzen Talraum und eine kleine Aufweitung mit Sitzbank lädt zum Verweilen ein. Der weitere Teil entlang der westlichen Grundstücksgrenze, führt dann auf den zentralen Platz, der Piazza genannt wird. Nicht nur diese Bezeichnung, sondern auch viele andere Elemente, wie das ziegelgedeckte Dach, aber auch die Gartengestaltung, stellen Bezüge zum südlichen Italien her.

Eine weitere Möglichkeit, diese 10 Meter tiefer gelegene Ebene zu erreichen, ist der große Aufzug, von dem aus man über die Alltagsgarage ebenso zur Piazza gelangt. Eine Raumkante dieser Piazza ist die verglaste Front der Garage, die sonst komplett erdüberdeckt und bewachsen ist. Der großzügige Garagenraum nimmt die Sammlung klassischer Automobile auf und ermöglicht auch die Sicht auf diese Schmuckstücke, sofern sie nicht durch eine Vorhanganlage, die von überall aus bedient werden kann, verborgen werden.

An der Südseite der Piazza schließt der loftartige, großzügige Wohnraum an, der über seine raumhohen Verglasungen einerseits eng mit dem Hof verbunden ist und auf der anderen Seite einen Panorama-Ausblick über die Stadt bietet. Im Sommer kann dieser Wohnraum dank großer Schiebetüren in den Innenhof erweitert werden. Über die Piazza kann der Architektur- und Kunstliebhaber auch auf kurzem Weg zu seiner Sammlung klassischer Porsche Sport- und Rennwagen gelangen. Die Autos können dort oder auf der Piazza für die Teilnahme an Klassik-Rennen vorbereitet werden, einer großen Passion des Bauherrn.

Ein Geschoss tiefer sind die privaten Schlafräume und Bäder und eine weitere Etage darunter gibt es einen großen offenen Atelierraum, der als Arbeitsraum und Büro genutzt wird, aber auch später für Freizeit, Hobby oder als Gästeapartment dienen kann.
Dank der Lage am Hang ist auch noch von dieser Ebene aus der Blick übers ganze Tal gegeben.

The residence for a Porsche enthusiast and car collector is located on a steep slope overlooking the city of Stuttgart.
Like the first house built for the same client in 1998, which is located directly adjacent, it is situated below a panoramic road typical of Stuttgart.

At first, the access to the house runs parallel to the slope. Here, the view opens up over the house to the entire valley basin, and a small widened area with a bench invites people to linger. The way continues along the western property line and leads to a central square, the so-called piazza. It is not only this name, but also numerous other elements that make references to southern Italy, such as the tiled roof and the garden landscaping.

Another way to reach this level, which is located 10 metres below the street, is the large lift, which also provides access to the piazza via the everyday garage. One spatial delimitation of this piazza is the glazed front of the collector's garage, which is otherwise completely covered with soil and greenery. The generous garage space accommodates the classic car collection, its glazing affording views of these gems, provided they are not hidden by a curtain system that can be remotely operated from anywhere.

A loft-like, spacious living room adjoins the piazza on the south side; on the one hand, it is closely connected to the courtyard via its floor-to-ceiling glazing, and on the other, it offers a panoramic view of the city. In summer, this living space can be extended to embrace the patio thanks to large sliding doors. Crossing the piazza is also the shortest way for the architecture and art lover to get to his collection of classic Porsche sports and racing cars. Here or on the piazza, the cars can be prepared for participation in classic car races, a great passion of the client.

The private bedrooms and bathrooms are located one floor below, while another floor further down features a large open studio space that is used as a workroom and office, but can later also serve for recreation, hobbies, or as a guest apartment.
Owing to the hillside location, views across the entire valley are also possible from this level.

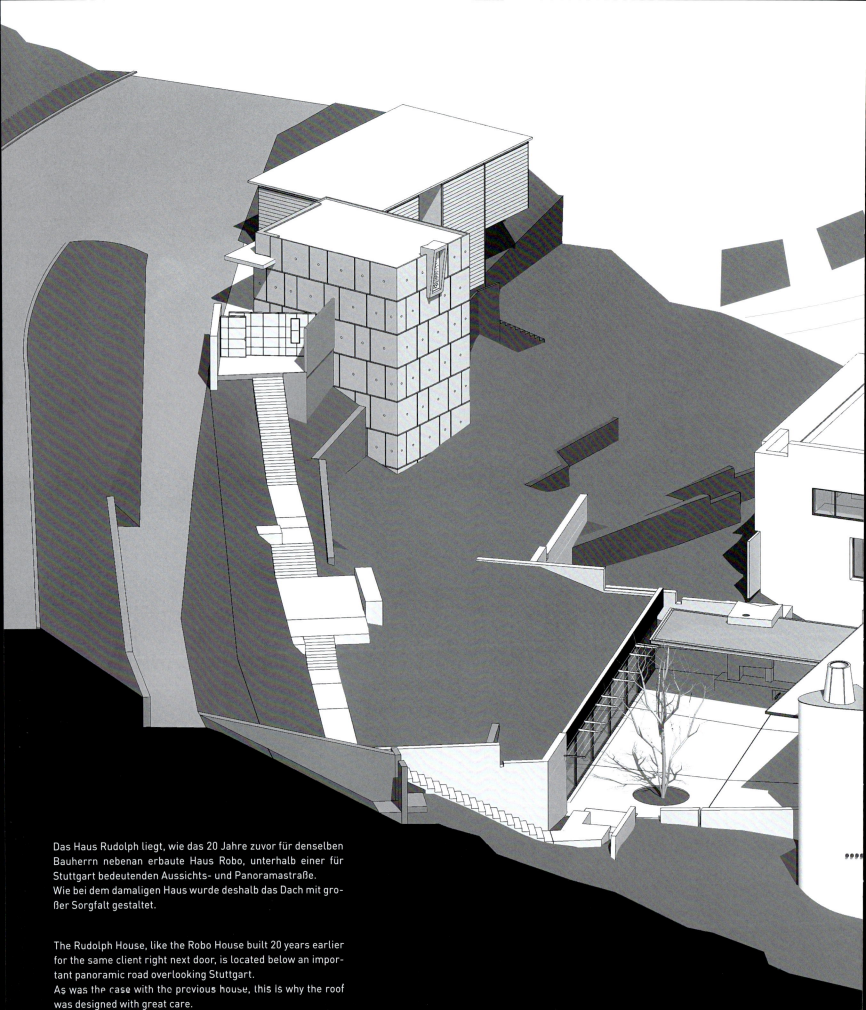

Das Haus Rudolph liegt, wie das 20 Jahre zuvor für denselben Bauherrn nebenan erbaute Haus Robo, unterhalb einer für Stuttgart bedeutenden Aussichts- und Panoramastraße.
Wie bei dem damaligen Haus wurde deshalb das Dach mit großer Sorgfalt gestaltet.

The Rudolph House, like the Robo House built 20 years earlier for the same client right next door, is located below an important panoramic road overlooking Stuttgart.
As was the case with the previous house, this is why the roof was designed with great care.

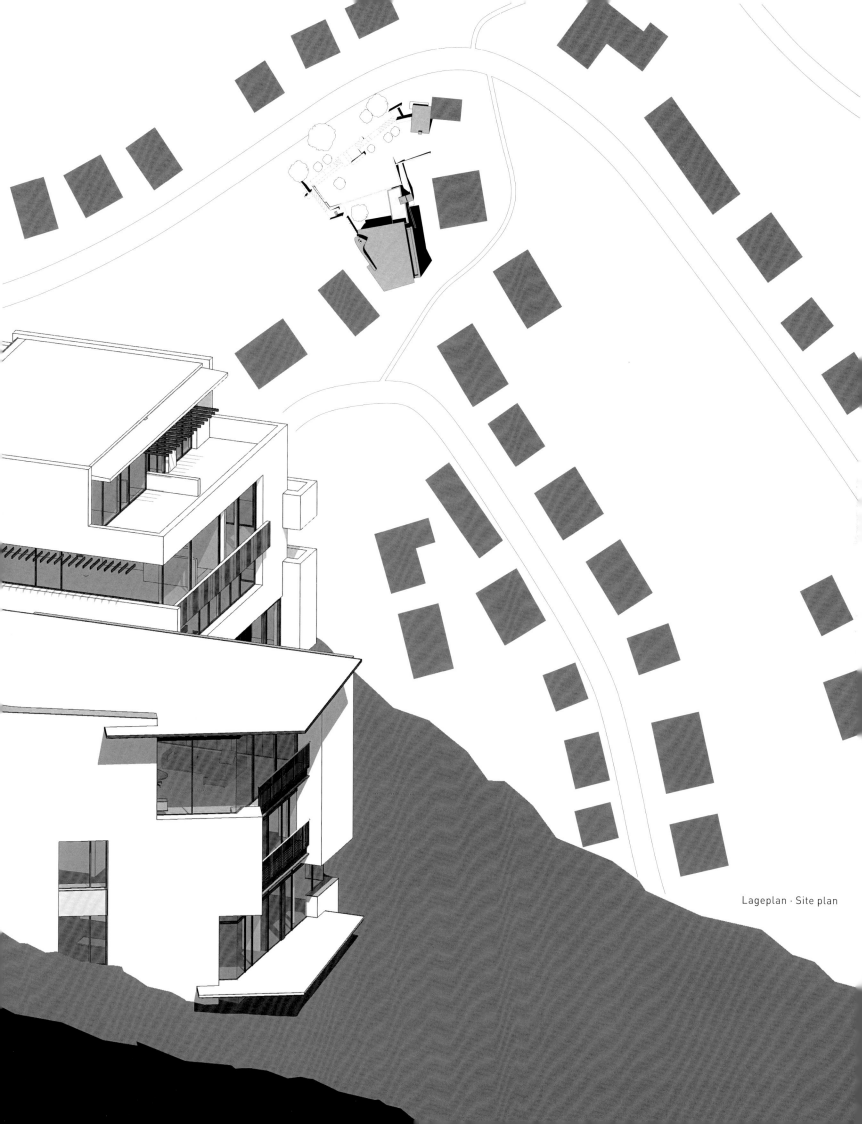

Lageplan · Site plan

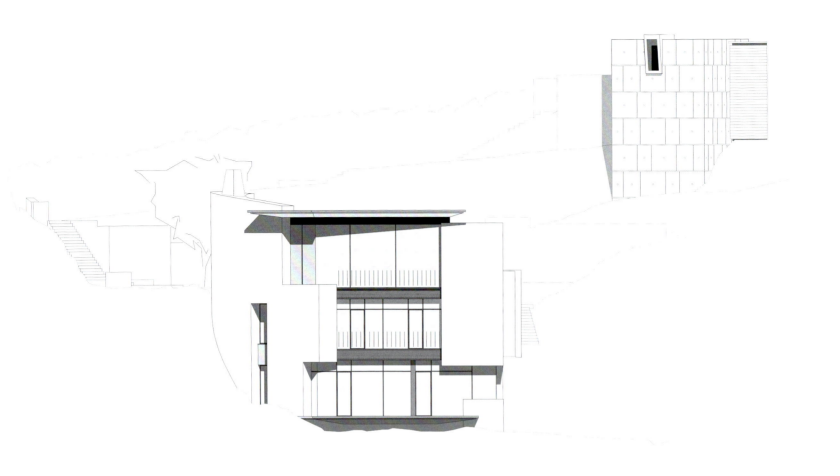

Ansicht Süd mit dem Turm des Auto-Aufzugs · South elevation with the tower of the car lift

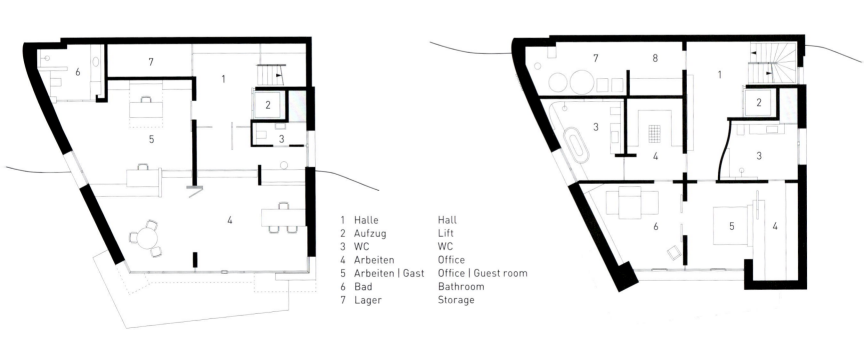

1 Halle — Hall
2 Aufzug — Lift
3 WC — WC
4 Arbeiten — Office
5 Arbeiten | Gast — Office | Guest room
6 Bad — Bathroom
7 Lager — Storage

Arbeiten · **Level 1** · Office

Schlafgeschoss · **Level 2** · Sleeping

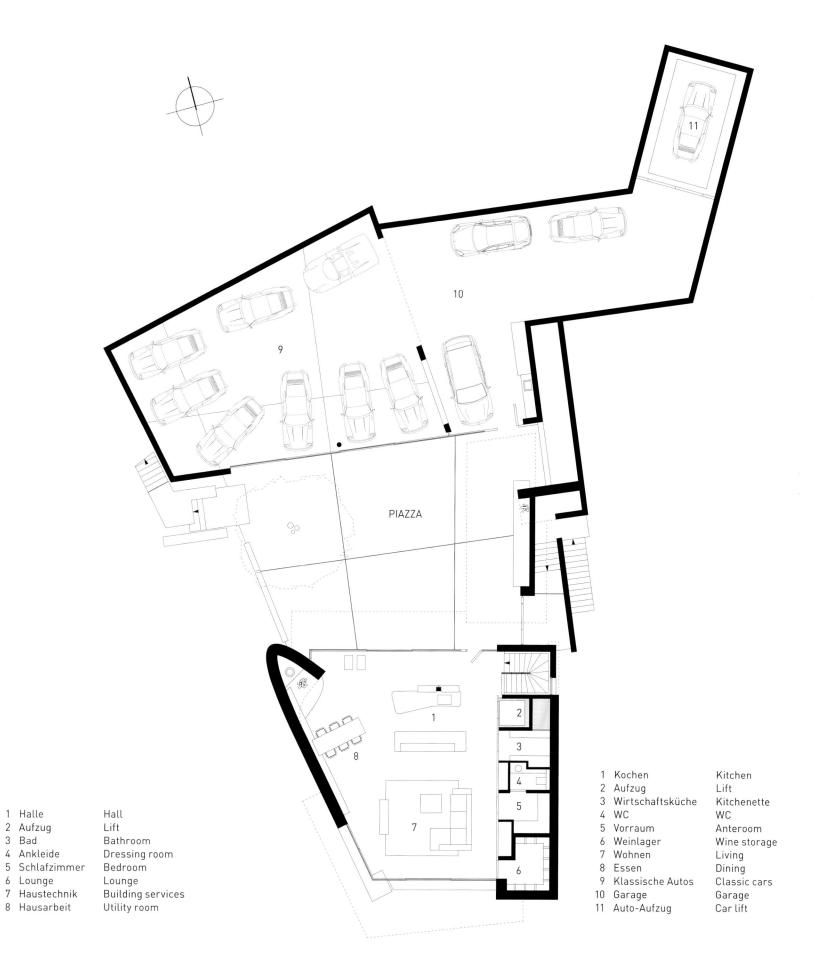

Haupt-Lebensraum · **Level 3** · Main Living Space

Die Piazza ist eine Oase der Ruhe, ganz nah an der Stadt, aber mit ihrem Fenster in die Natur doch ganz weit weg von dieser. Die dreiseitigen Platzwände erinnern uns an bekannte und vertraute Räume. Mit der Öffnung der Piazza nach Westen, zur Abendsonne hin und mit der großen Catalpa als beschirmendes Element wird sie zum erträumten sommerlichen Außenraum.

The piazza is an oasis of tranquillity, very close to the city, yet, with its window facing nature, very far away from it.
The piazza walls on three sides recall familiar and trusted spaces. Opening up the piazza to the west, towards the evening sun, and the large catalpa as a shading element turn it into a dreamt-of outdoor space in summer.

Schon wie beim danebenstehenden Vorgängerbau aus dem Jahr 1998 ist für den städtischen Flaneur das Dach die Hauptansicht.
Da der Bauherr eine große Affinität zu Süditalien und Capri hat, finden sich am Haus, im Garten, aber vor allem in der Dachlandschaft Bilder aus dieser Region wieder.

As with the first house built next door in 1998, the roof is the main elevation for people looking at the city. Since both the client and the architect have a great affection for southern Italy and Capri, images from this region can be found in the house, in the garden, but especially in the roofscape.

Schon während der Bauzeit gab es von verschiedenen Zeitschriften Interesse am zukünftigen Ort der Sammlung des Bauherrn.
So fanden dann auch noch vor Fertigstellung der Gebäude Fotoshootings dort statt.
Dabei entstanden auch diese Bilder des Stuttgarter Fotografen Max Leitner.

Even during the construction period, various magazines expressed interest in the future location of the client's collection.
Hence, photo shoots took place there even before the buildings were completed.
The pictures by photographer Max Leitner from Stuttgart were also taken here.

  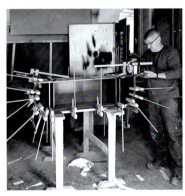

Wir lieben es, mit guten, wachen und erfahrenen Handwerkern zu arbeiten, gemeinsame Antworten auf unsere Ideen zu finden und das Projekt unter ihren Händen Stück für Stück erstrahlen zu lassen. Wir alle glauben daran, dass auf diese Weise das besondere architektonische Werk entsteht und es sich lohnt, diesen Weg gemeinsam zu gehen.

We love to work with good, alert and experienced craftsmen, to find common answers to our ideas and to let the project shine through the work of their hands, step by step. We all firmly believe that this is how the special architectural work is created, and it is worthwhile to take this path together.

Wünsche und Träume unserer Bauherrschaft zu realisieren ist uns ein Anliegen und oft können wir dadurch, dass wir alle Möbel und Einbauten entwerfen und konstruieren, auch ungewöhnliche Kombinationen umsetzen. So konnten wir hier unter dem Arbeitstisch des Alltags ein DJ-Pult integrieren, das vielleicht selten, aber dafür umso mehr Freude bereitet.

Making our clients' wishes and dreams come true is of great concern to us; and as we design and construct all the furniture and built-in units ourselves, we are often able to implement unusual combinations. Here, for example, we managed to integrate a DJ console underneath the desktop used on a daily basis; perhaps it is enjoyed only rarely, but all the more for that.

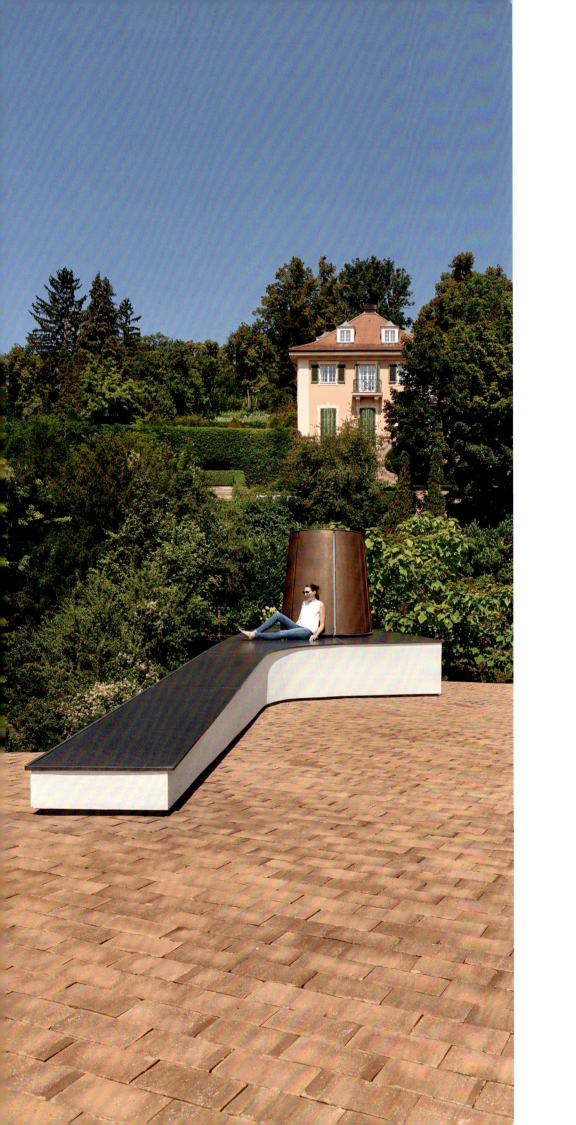

Die Wirklichkeit der Architektur ist nicht die gebaute. Es ist die Kraft der Bilder.   The reality of architecture is not the built one. It is the power of images.

In den weiten und 3,30 Meter hohen Wohnbereich wurde ein Kubus eingestellt, der zur einen Seite die Küchenrückwand ist und auf der anderen Seite eine Wohn- und Bücherwand. Er gliedert den fließenden Raum in unterschiedliche Bereiche, aber die lange Wand aus schwarzem Stahl, die Böden, die Decke und das Sideboard mit ihren homogenen Oberflächen halten alles im Fluss. Die gerundeten Ecken am Küchenblock, ebenfalls aus rohem Stahl, erleichtern die arbeitsame Bewegung um ihn herum.

A cube was placed in the large living area with a ceiling height of 3.30 metres, which serves as the rear wall of the kitchen area on one side and as a wall and bookshelf facing the living room on the other. It divides the continuous space into different areas, but the long black steel wall, the floors, the ceiling and the sideboard with their homogeneous surfaces keep everything flowing.
The rounded corners of the kitchen unit, also made of raw steel, facilitate the laborious activity around it.

FINEWAY HOUSE
PRIVATE RESIDENTIAL CASTLE, REUTLINGEN
2019

Das Fineway House liegt unterhalb einer Wohnstraße, die als Spazierweg entlang der Achalm sehr beliebt ist. Um von dort den Ausblick auf den Albtrauf zu erhalten, liegt das Haus mit seiner Oberkante tiefer als die öffentliche Erschließung.
Um hier Einblicke zu vermeiden, ist die hangseitige Fassade weitgehend geschlossen. Ihr vorgelagert ist ein Hof, der von einem kühn geschwungenen Dach überspannt wird und mit der Wand des Garagenkörpers einen ganz besonderen Außenraum bildet.
Der direkte Zugang von der Wirtschaftsküche ermöglicht dort ein Frühstück in der Morgensonne und bietet vor allem an heißen Sommertagen einen schattigen und luftigen Sitzplatz.
Auch die Pflege der Hobbys und alle anderen Aktivitäten sind hier denkbar und durch die ruhige Gestaltung des Garagenbauwerks ist dieser Platz mehr Lebensraum als Erschließungsfläche.

Über den Haupteingang gelangt man direkt in den Wohnbereich, an den sich hinter einem raumgliedernden Kaminkörper Essen und Kochen anschließt. Auf der anderen Seite gelangt man an der Halle vorbei in die privaten Räume der Bewohner.
So erweist sich dieses Haus in der Benutzung eher als eingeschossiger Bungalow, der lediglich im Sockel auf der Talseite um zusätzliche Nutzungen ergänzt wird. Hier sind neben der Technik ein Spa-Bereich, aber auch ein Arbeitszimmer und ein Gäste-Apartment untergebracht.

Das Bild des Hauses entstand aus dem Ort selbst, seiner Lage in der Landschaft, direkt unterhalb der Burg Achalm aus dem 11. Jahrhundert, von der lediglich der 14 Meter hohe Bergfried erhalten ist. Es ist also eine Art „Wiederaufbau" der restlichen Burg an anderer Stelle. Dennoch orientiert sich dieses Werk nicht an der mittelalterlichen Bauweise, sondern ist eher als zeitgemäße „humanistische Burg" gedacht, die aber auch schon vor Längerem aus der Erde gewachsen sein könnte. Roh und grob, aber auch fein und leicht. Seine einfache Schönheit steht wie selbstverständlich und standhaft in der Landschaft.

Fineway House is also located below a residential street. This street, in turn, is a very popular footpath along the Achalm hill.
In order to preserve the view of the escarpment of the Swabian Alps, the upper edge of the house is lower than the public road.
In order to avoid views into the building, the façade facing the slope has only few openings. In front of it is a courtyard covered by a boldly curved roof which, together with the garage wall, forms a very special outdoor space.
Thanks to the direct access from the utility kitchen, this area is a great place to have breakfast in the morning sun and, especially on hot summer days, a shady and airy place to sit.
Indulging in hobbies and many other activities are also conceivable here; and the calm design of the garage building makes this place more of a living space than a circulation area.

The main entrance leads directly into the living area, which is adjoined by the dining and cooking areas behind a room-dividing volume accommodating a fireplace. On the other side, the residents reach their private rooms after passing the hall.
Thus, in terms of use, this house rather resembles a one-storey bungalow with additional uses in the plinth on the side facing the valley. In addition to building services, this level accommodates a spa area, a study and a guest apartment.

The appearance of the house originated from the location itself, its position in the landscape, directly below the 11th century Achalm Castle, of which only the 14-metres-high keep is preserved. It is therefore a kind of "reconstruction" of the castle remains in a different place. Nevertheless, this project is not based on medieval architecture, but is rather intended as a contemporary "humanistic castle", which, however, could also have grown from the ground a long time ago. Raw and rough, but also delicate and light. Its plain beauty sits naturally and steadfastly in the landscape.

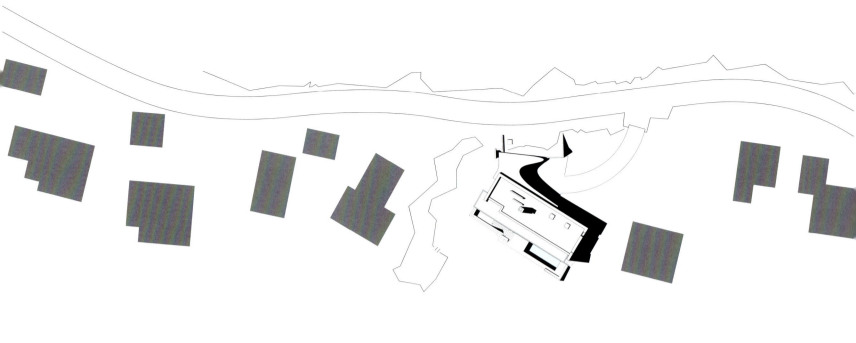

Lageplan · Site plan

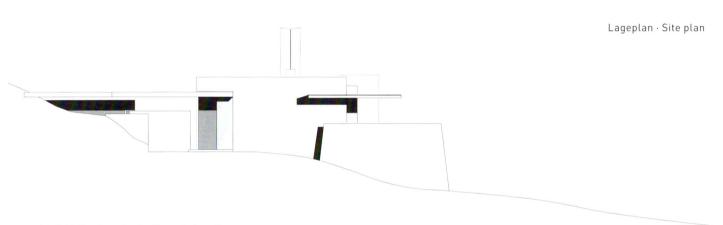

Ansicht Nordwest · Northwest elevation

1 Haustechnik — Building services
2 Abstellraum — Storeroom
3 Sauna | Fitness — Sauna | Fitness
4 Halle — Hall
5 Weinkeller — Wine cellar
6 Arbeiten — Study
7 Gast — Guest room
8 Pool — Pool

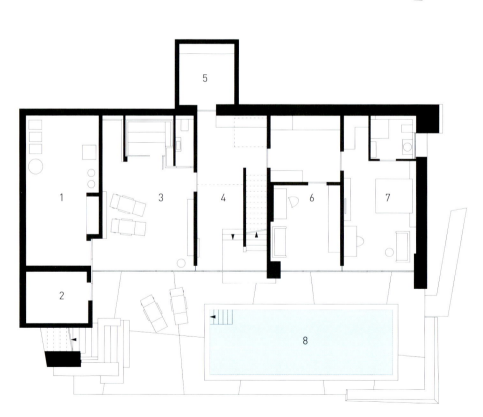

Spa und Gast · **Level 1** · Spa and guest

0 — 5m

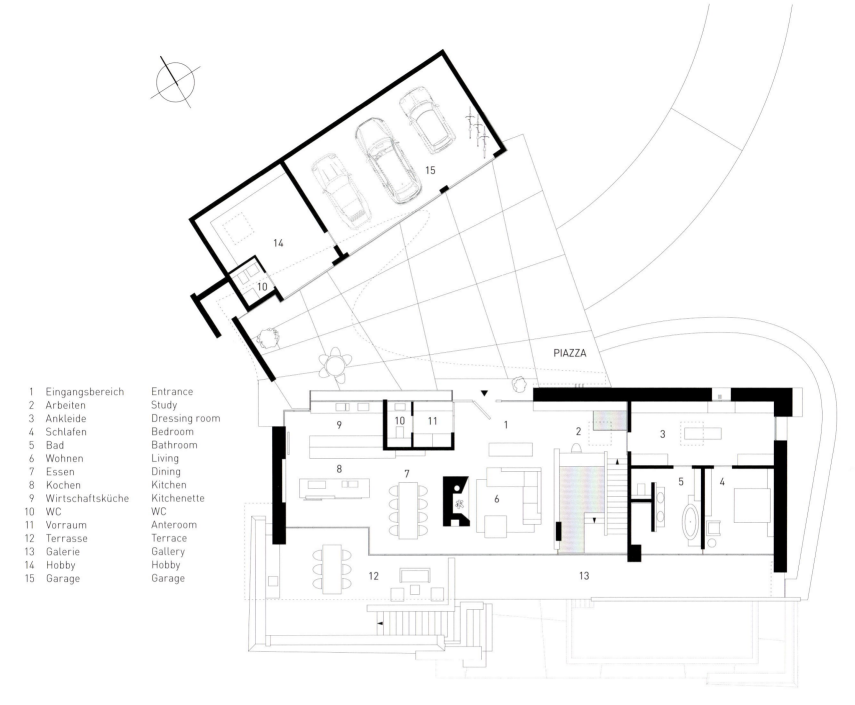

1	Eingangsbereich	Entrance
2	Arbeiten	Study
3	Ankleide	Dressing room
4	Schlafen	Bedroom
5	Bad	Bathroom
6	Wohnen	Living
7	Essen	Dining
8	Kochen	Kitchen
9	Wirtschaftsküche	Kitchenette
10	WC	WC
11	Vorraum	Anteroom
12	Terrasse	Terrace
13	Galerie	Gallery
14	Hobby	Hobby
15	Garage	Garage

Haupt-Wohngeschoss · **Level 2** · Main residential floor

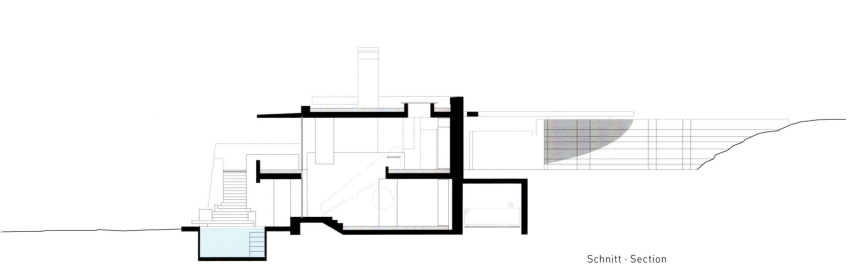

Schnitt · Section

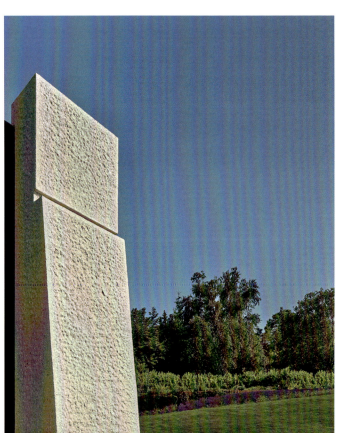

Viele Gegenstände, die unseren Alltag prägen, haben für uns eine eindeutige Identität, welche durch ihren Gebrauch bestimmt wird. An einen solchen Gegenstand haben wir dann meist keine weiteren Fragen.
Unser Ziel ist es, den einzelnen Bauteilen eine Persönlichkeit zu geben, die über den eigentlichen Nutzwert hinausgeht und wie hier beispielsweise auch Sitz- und Aufenthaltsqualität bietet.
Im Idealfall gelingt es, ein Werk als Monolith zu konstruieren, das auch außerhalb seiner Funktion der Sinnlichkeit und Schönheit verpflichtet ist, vergleichbar der autonomen Poesie einer Skulptur.

Many objects that are part of our everyday life have a clear identity for us, which is determined by their utility value. We usually have no further questions about such objects.
Our aim is to give the individual components a personality that goes beyond their actual utility value and, as in this case, additionally offers a great quality for sitting down and lingering.
Ideally, we succeed in constructing a building as a monolith that, even beyond its function, depicts a built reality that is committed to sensuality and beauty, comparable to the autonomous poetry of a sculpture.

Die Welt, in der wir heute leben, ist gekennzeichnet von Vermengungen und Vermischungen von Stoffen bis zu deren Unkenntlichkeit. Im täglichen Baugeschehen setzen sich die Gebäudeteile oft aus einer Unzahl von verbundenen, verklebten und abgedichteten Einzelteilen zusammen.
Diesem Umstand wollen wir mit einer monolithischen Bauweise entgegentreten.
Der stabile und beständige Beton ermöglicht ein dauerhaftes Verbleiben des Bauwerks.
Feste Steinhäuser, die auch noch nach Jahrhunderten ihren Dienst tun, sind hier unsere Referenz.

Diese Bauweise ermöglicht auch ein direktes Erwachsen des Hauses aus dem Boden, ohne dass hier weitere Maßnahmen erforderlich wären.
Hier begegnen sich das Tun des Menschen und die Erde unmittelbar.

The world we live in today is characterised by the blending and mixing of materials to the point of being unrecognisable. In everyday construction activities, building components are often made up of a myriad of connected, glued and sealed individual parts.
We want to counteract this situation with monolithic construction.
Robust and durable concrete allows the building to remain permanently and prolongs its natural cycle. Solid stone houses that still serve their purpose after centuries are our reference for this.

Concrete also allows the building to grow directly from the ground without the need to take any further measures.
Here, the activities of man and the earth come into direct contact.

Das Haus entsteht aus dem Zusammenwirken einzelner architektonischer Teile. Entsprechend ihrer Position im Raum verbergen sie dahinterliegende Funktionen und technische Einrichtungen, die für den Besucher oder im Alltag nur untergeordnete Bedeutung haben. Die monochromen und gleichmäßigen Oberflächen der Einzelelemente strukturieren und ordnen den Raum. Die Unterschiedlichkeit und die Materialvielfalt dieser Einzelelemente ermöglicht ein weiteres Hinzufügen, eben auch des Unbestimmten.

The house emerges from the interaction of individual architectural parts. Depending on their position in the room, they conceal functions and technical installations behind them that are of only secondary importance for the visitor or in everyday life. The monochrome and uniform surfaces of the individual elements structure and order the space. The diversity and variety of materials of these individual elements allows for further additions, including the indeterminate.

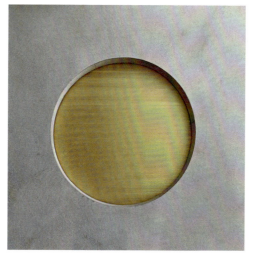

In vollem Sonnenschein bis unter die dunkle Klarheit des Mondes spricht der Stein mit immer anderen Worten, aber dem gleichen Sinn. Dem Menschen das Bedürfnis nach Schönheit, Kunst und Poesie zurückzugeben, heißt, ihm seine Natur wiederzuschenken.

In bright sunlight or in the dark clarity of the moon, stone expresses itself with ever different words, but always the same meaning. Returning to man the need for beauty, art and poetry means giving man back his nature.

Das gebaute Haus sollte die Natur nicht nachahmen, sondern weiterführen. Es sollte frei von Fesseln sein und letztendlich das individuelle Sinnes- und Gefühlsleben des Menschen in sich tragen. Zumindest sollte es ein sinnverwandter Freund sein.

The built house should not imitate nature but continue it. It should be free of fetters and ultimately bear within itself the individual sensory and emotional life of the human being. A congenial friend, at least.

BRENNER RESEARCH HOUSE
PRIVATE RESIDENCE AND ATELIER, STUTTGART
2018

An den Stuttgarter Hängen wird seit über 100 Jahren nach dem Ortsbaustatut gebaut. Auch die ergänzenden Baustaffeln 8 oder 7 geben eine Überbauung der Grundfläche von 20 bis 25 Prozent vor. Diese städtebauliche Grundidee geht ursprünglich auf Theodor Fischer zurück und sollte zu grünen Hängen führen, die die dichte Stadt umgeben.

Als zeitgemäße Fortführung der an den Hängen entstandenen klassischen Stuttgarter Kaffeemühlen auf meist quadratischem Grundriss wurde dieses Haus erdacht, aber es sollte auch zugleich ein Gegenentwurf zu den heute üblichen Bauweisen werden.
Es entstand als „Research House", bei dem, frei von Dogmen und Ideologien die Verbindung traditioneller Bauweisen mit neuen Möglichkeiten und Techniken untersucht wurden.
Gleichzeitig ist es eine gebaute Autobiografie, also eine Zusammenschau aus 30 Jahren Baupraxis. Darüber hinaus wollten wir hier weitere zukünftige Bauweisen unseres Ateliers entwickeln und erproben. Somit steht es für den Aufbruch zu einer noch stärkeren Gewichtung des Dauerhaften und Haltbaren und damit des Nachhaltigen im eigentlichen Wortsinn, wie wir es verstehen.
Auch deshalb wurde auf zeittypische, scheinbar unumgängliche industrielle Produkte und übliche Regelbauweisen verzichtet, so vor allem auf Kunststoffe, Verbundbaustoffe, Verklebungen und Ausschäumungen. Alle Materialien, die am Haus verwendet wurden, zeichnen sich dadurch aus, dass sie in reiner Form mit ihren natürlichen, unbehandelten und unversiegelten Oberflächen verarbeitet wurden.
Die Außenwände aus 25 Zentimeter starkem, bearbeitetem Beton und dahinterliegenden 48 Zentimeter dicken Porenbetonwänden schließen das Haus zum Hang hin dreiseitig ab. Wenige akzentuierte Öffnungen und senkrechte, massive Wände lassen es hier fast wie eine Burg erscheinen, wohingegen die Südostseite eine starke Differenzierung in Material und Tiefe erfährt.

Vom Straßenniveau bis zum Dachgeschoss sind es fünf Ebenen, die über wechselnde Treppen erschlossen werden. Oberhalb der Eingangsebene ist das offene Ateliergeschoss und darüberliegend, auf der dritten Ebene, Schlafraum, Bad und Ankleide. Zugunsten der besseren Aussicht ist das „Lebensgeschoss" mit Küche, Essen und Kaminecke auf der vierten Ebene, und hier schließt auch das rückseitige Gartenzimmer an. Bibliothek, Arbeiten und Kontemplation mit vorgelagerter Dachterrasse finden sich dann ganz oben, auf der fünften Ebene.

For more than 100 years, building on Stuttgart's hillsides has been subject to building bylaws, first the so-called Ortsbaustatut and later Baustaffel 8 or 7. These local regulations stipulate that the building footprint must not exceed 20-25% of the site area. This basic urban planning idea goes back to Theodor Fischer and was aimed at creating green slopes around the dense city.

This house was conceived as a contemporary continuation of the classic detached, cube-shaped residences in Stuttgart, but it was also intended to be a counter-design to the currently common construction methods.
That is why it became a "Research House", where, free of dogmas and ideologies, the combination of traditional building methods with new possibilities and techniques are investigated.
At the same time, it is a built autobiography, that is, a synopsis of 30 years of building practice. In addition, we wanted this project to develop and test further future building methods of our studio. Hence it is a departure towards an even stronger emphasis on durability and longevity and thus on sustainability in the true sense of the word and as we understand it.
This is one of the reasons why we avoided the standard construction methods and seemingly indispensable industrial products typical of the time, especially plastics, composite building materials, adhesives and foams. All materials used for the building are distinguished by having been processed in their pure form with their natural, untreated and unsealed surfaces.
The 25 cm thick concrete exterior walls and the 48 cm thick aerated concrete walls behind them enclose the house on three sides towards the slope. With only a few accentuated openings and vertical, solid walls, this section almost looks like a castle, whereas the south-east side is marked by a strong differentiation in terms of material and depth.

From the street level up to the attic, the building comprises five levels, which are accessed via varying stairs. Above the entrance level is the open studio floor, while the third level accommodates the bedroom, bathroom and dressing room. In favour of a better view, the main living area with kitchen, dining area, a fireplace with a sitting area next to it and the garden room adjoining at the back is located on the fourth level. The fifth level features a library, study and contemplation area with a roof terrace at the front.

Lageplan · Site plan

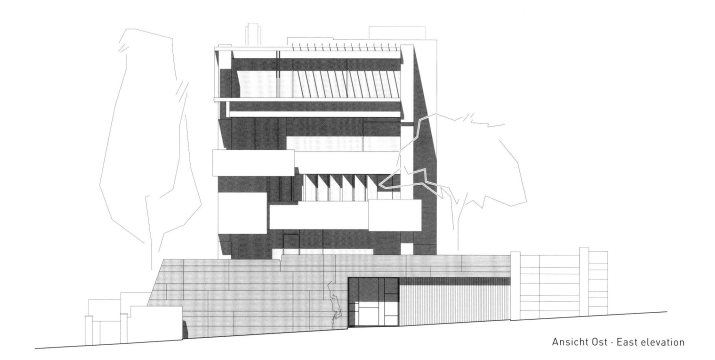

Ansicht Ost · East elevation

Ansicht Nord · North elevation

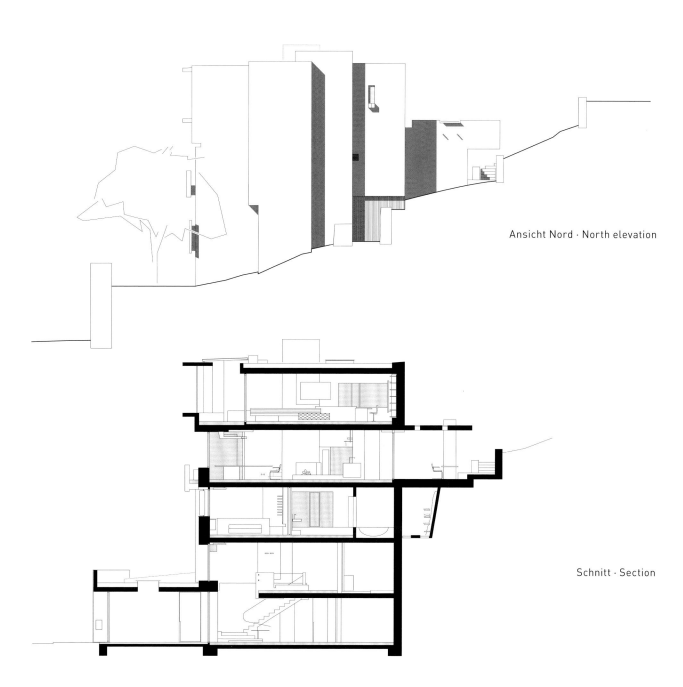

Schnitt · Section

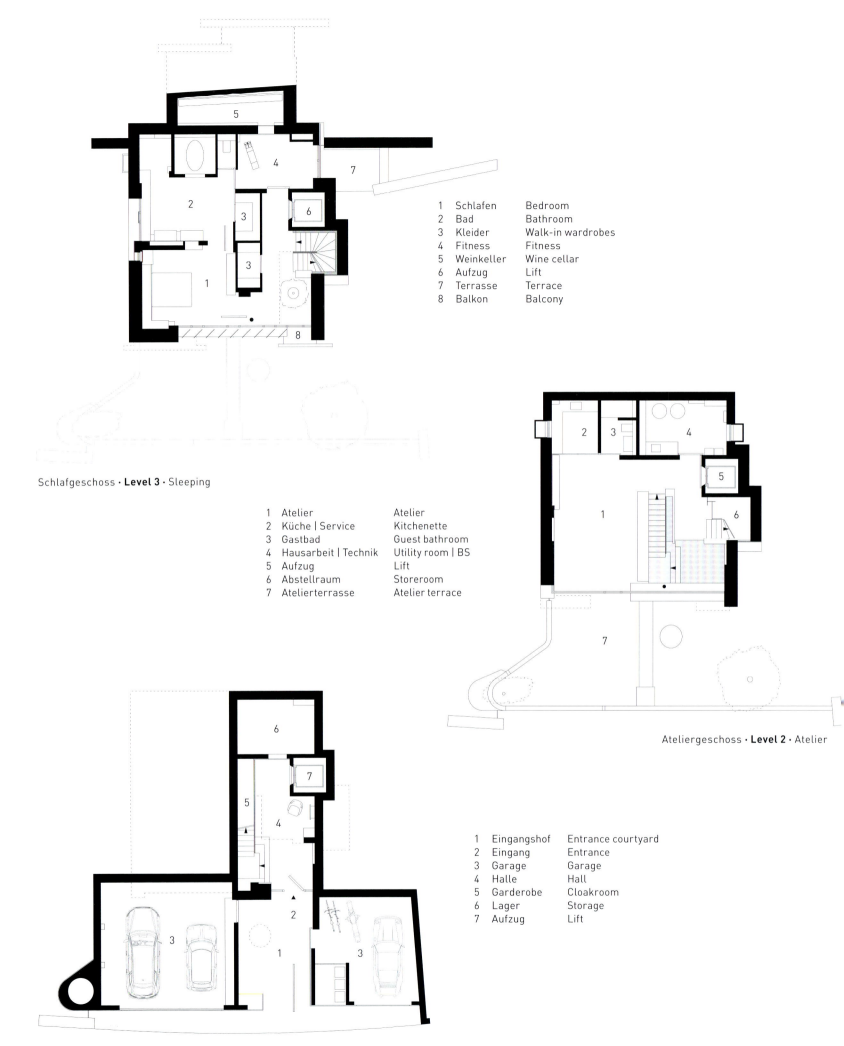

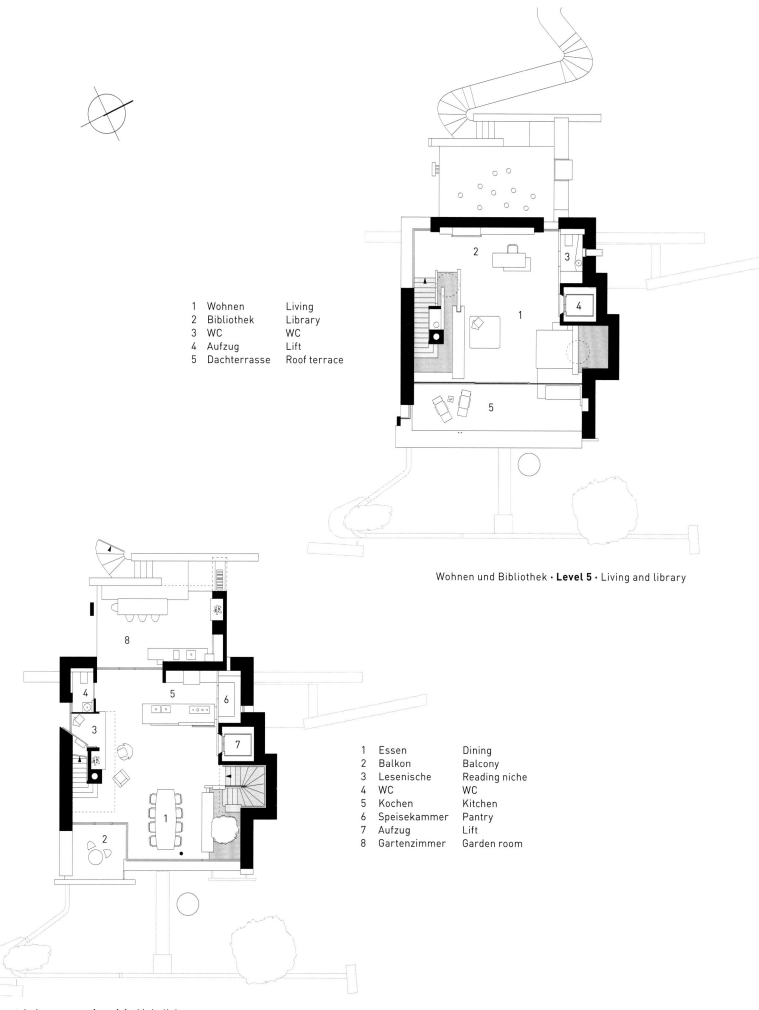

1	Wohnen	Living
2	Bibliothek	Library
3	WC	WC
4	Aufzug	Lift
5	Dachterrasse	Roof terrace

Wohnen und Bibliothek · **Level 5** · Living and library

1	Essen	Dining
2	Balkon	Balcony
3	Lesenische	Reading niche
4	WC	WC
5	Kochen	Kitchen
6	Speisekammer	Pantry
7	Aufzug	Lift
8	Gartenzimmer	Garden room

Haupt-Lebensraum · **Level 4** · Main living space

Die Sichtbetonwände erscheinen dank des verwendeten lokalen Jurasplitts in warmem Graubeige.
Durch das grobe Spitzen und Stocken der Betonhaut wirkt dieser Stadtbaustein wie ein Fels, bekommt aber gleichzeitig durch zahlreiche Vor- und Rücksprünge und das steinmetzmäßige Scharrieren der Kanten und Brüstungen eine hohe Feinheit und Präzision.
Glatt geschalte Betonbrüstungen, geglättete Oberflächen und tiefe Einschnitte differenzieren die offene südöstliche Straßenfassade und führen zum gewünschten tiefen Bild.

Owing to the added local Jura chippings, the exposed concrete walls appear in a warm grey-beige shade.
Rough chiselling and bush hammering of the concrete envelope gives this urban element the appearance of a rock, but at the same time the numerous protrusions and recesses and the stonemasonry-like chiselling of the edges and parapets lend it a high degree of refinement and precision.
Smooth-formed concrete parapets, polished surfaces and deep recesses differentiate the open southeast street façade and result in the desired deep appearance.

Durch die beim Brenner Research House gewählte Konstruktion mit allen außen liegenden Bauteilen in Sichtbeton, bekommt die sorgfältige Ausführung des Rohbaus große Bedeutung.
Wir sind deshalb glücklich und dankbar dafür, dass wir Baumeister, die für ihr außerordentliches Können in der Betonverarbeitung bekannt sind, dazu gewinnen konnten, die bisher geglaubten Grenzen des Machbaren noch ein Stückchen weiter zu verschieben.

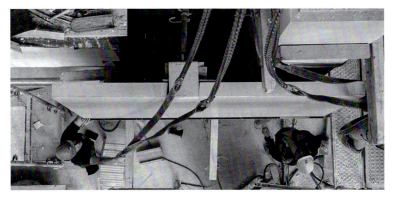

Due to the construction method chosen for the Brenner Research House, i.e. using fair-faced concrete for all external components, the building shell and its careful execution are of the utmost importance.
We are therefore happy and grateful that we were able to convince master builders, who are known for their extraordinary skills in concrete processing, to push the limits of what was previously believed to be possible just a little further.

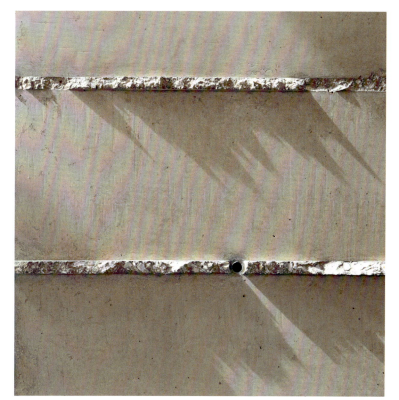

Schon die Römer erschufen ihre dauerhaftesten und anspruchsvollsten Bauwerke mit Opus Caementitium, einer frühen Form des Betons. Nach vielen Jahren des Bauens weißer Häuser entstand bei mir der drängende Wunsch nach noch dauerhafteren Wänden, die auch ohne überstehende Dächer auskommen könnten. Deshalb haben wir über Jahre an Beton als Wandmaterial geforscht und dies hauptsächlich an der Witterung ausgesetzten Bauteilen. Dabei haben wir die Rezepturen, die Schalungen, die Zuschlagsstoffe und die anschließende Bearbeitung im Laufe der Zeit immer mehr optimiert.
Heute haben wir ein Team von besonderen Menschen zusammen, das vom Betonwerk über die perfekte Verarbeitung des Ortbetons bis zu den Steinmetzarbeiten alle Kompetenzen vereint.

The Romans already built their most durable and sophisticated structures from opus caementitium. After many years of designing white houses, I had the urgent desire for even more durable walls that could do without projecting roofs. For this reason, research was carried out over many years on concrete as a wall material, mainly on components exposed to the weather.
Over the years, the formulas, the formwork, the aggregates and the subsequent processing have been optimised.
Meanwhile, we have built a team of special people, whose expertise ranges from the concrete plant to the perfect processing of in-situ concrete to stonemasonry.

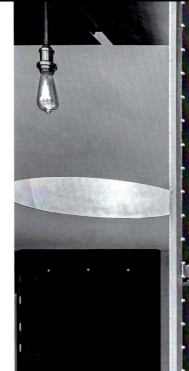

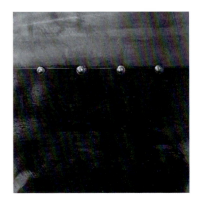

Wir alle wissen, dass das kunstvolle Bauwerk nicht das Werk von wenigen oder gar Einzelnen ist. Auch wenn wir alles planen und es letztendlich auch verantworten, so ist der Prozess immer ein kooperativer und gemeinsamer. Viele Male holen wir die Meinung der Ausführenden ein, mit denen wir oft über Jahrzehnte zusammenarbeiten.
Ein gutes Bauwerk entsteht aus den Fähigkeiten, dem Wissen und der Motivation aller Beteiligter.

We all know that the elaborate building is not the work of a few or even of an individual. Even though we plan everything and are ultimately responsible for it, the process is always one of cooperation and joint efforts; and frequently we seek the opinion of those who carry out the work, with whom we have often worked for decades, as is the case here.
A good building is the result of the skills, knowledge and motivation of all those involved.

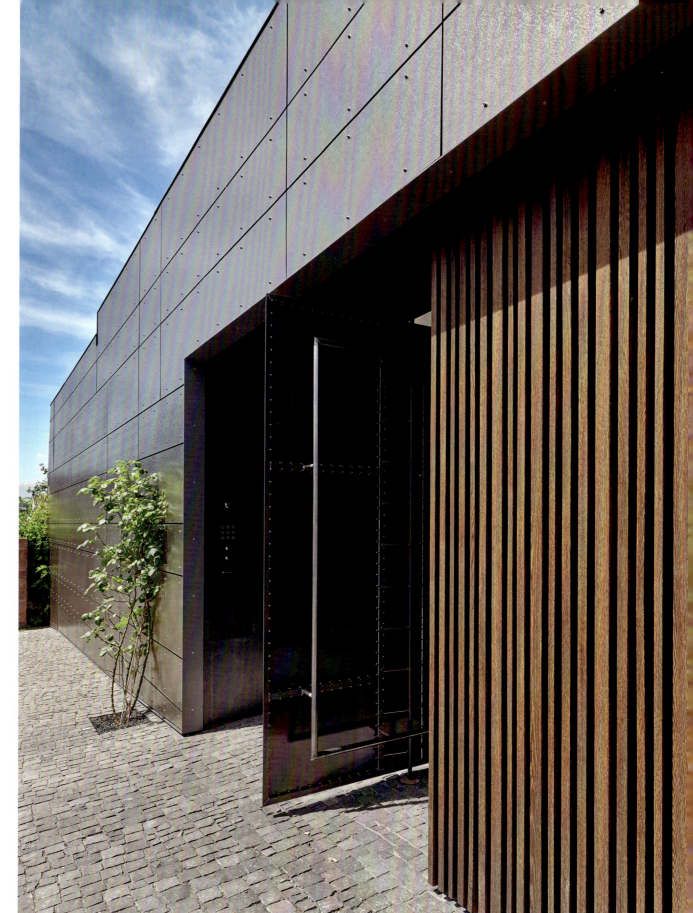

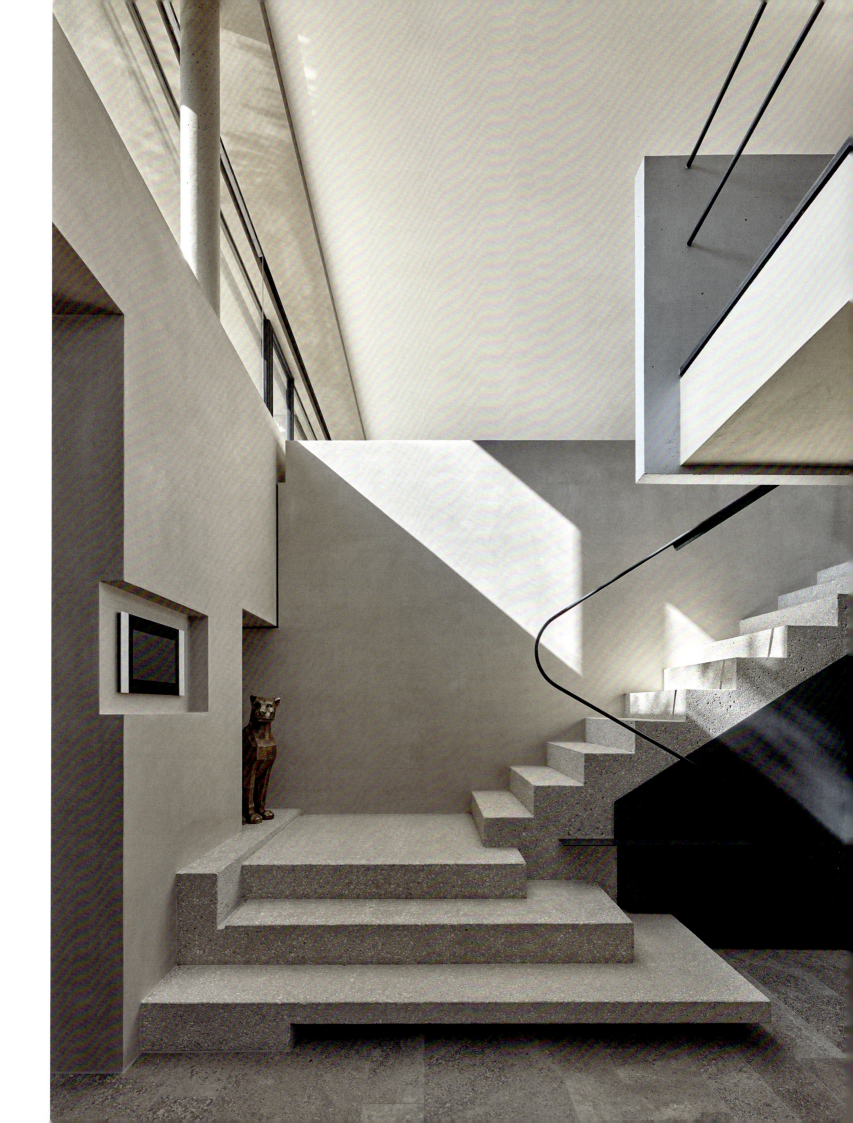

Wie hier im Ateliergeschoss wurden im ganzen Haus dauerhafte, aus der Region stammende, naturbelassene Baustoffe eingesetzt. Beispiele hierfür sind der reine Kalkputz ohne Anstrich, die unlackierten Holzflächen, teilweise geköhlte und recycelte Hölzer, Trittschalldämmung aus Holzweichfaser, lokaler Muschelkalkstein, Eichenboden aus einer jahrhundertealten, nachhaltigen Forstwirtschaft, Vollholzmöbel, Linoleum, unbehandeltes Messing und Stahl.
Auch wurde zugunsten der Dauerhaftigkeit weitgehend auf elektrische und motorbetriebene Anlagen verzichtet, und so sind Sonnenschutz und Verdunklung im Schlafgeschoss manuell zu bedienen.

As here on the studio level, durable, locally sourced, natural building materials were used throughout the house. Examples of this are the pure lime plaster without coating, the unpainted wooden surfaces, partially carbonised recycled wood, impact sound insulation made of soft wood fibre, local shell limestone, oak flooring from a centuries-old sustainable forestry, solid wood furniture, linoleum, untreated brass and steel.
In the interests of durability, electrical and motorised systems were largely dispensed with, so that sun protection and shading on the sleeping level are operated manually.

Auf der dritten Ebene hatte der hangseitige Spritzbetonverbau, der zur Grundstückssicherung notwendig war, einen solchen Abstand zum Haus, dass es möglich wurde, diesen Zwischenbereich, anstatt ihn wie üblich zu verfüllen, als Weinkeller zu nutzen.
Die Lage des Kellers außerhalb des Hauses und tief im Erdreich sorgt hier für eine konstante Temperatur. Er ist wie die Keller in früheren Zeiten mit einem offenen Boden versehen, so dass auch die Luftfeuchtigkeit und der Geruch an längst verloren Geglaubtes erinnert. Zwei hintereinanderliegende Massivholztüren isolieren und trennen ihn vom Wohnhaus.

On the third level, the shotcrete shoring system, which was necessary to support the slope, is at such a distance from the house that it became possible to use this in-between space as a wine cellar instead of filling it in as usual.
The cellar's location outside the house and deep in the ground ensures a constant room temperature. Like the cellars in earlier times, it has an unsealed floor, so that the humidity and the smell are reminiscent of things believed to have been lost long ago. Two solid wooden doors, one behind the other, insulate and separate the cellar from the house.

Die heutige Vorstellung von der klassischen Moderne ist davon geprägt, dass es kein Dekor, kein unnötiges Zierrat oder gar figurative Elemente geben dürfe. Viele sinnliche Elemente und gerade auch spielerische Details und Feinheiten sind deshalb heute aus dem Architekturgeschehen verschwunden.
Solche Elemente und Details, teils auch augenzwinkernd, finden sich hier aber als Türgriffe, Ausstattungsgegenstände oder als reine Installation, symbolhaft gestaltet, mit Motiven aus der Mensch- und Tierwelt oder als historisches Zitat im ganzen Haus wieder. Auch die Wiedereinführung der Intarsie als massives Messing-Inlay im Boden soll das Herz und die Seele der Besucher erfreuen.
Es ist der Versuch, die verlorene Einheit wiederzugewinnen, die einerseits im strengen Akademikertum und andererseits in kunstgewerblichen Kitsch zugrunde gegangen scheint.

Today's idea of Classical Modernism is characterised by the notion that there should be no decoration and no unnecessary ornamentation or even figurative elements. Many sensual elements and especially playful details and subtleties have therefore disappeared from architectural practice to this day.
Such elements and details, sometimes tongue-in-cheek, can be found throughout the house as door handles, items of equipment or as pure installations – with symbolical design, with motifs from the human and animal worlds or as historical references. The reintroduction of the inlay in the form of a solid brass inlay in the floor is also intended to warm the hearts and souls of visitors.
It is an attempt to regain the lost unity that seems to have perished in strict academia on the one hand and in arts-and-crafts kitsch on the other.

Einige Einbauten im Haus lagern auf Grundkonstruktionen aus Beton, die schon im Rohbau erstellt wurden. So ist es auch hier beim Küchentresen, der mit Kupferblech beschlagen wurde. In die Arbeitsfläche aus strukturiertem Edelstahl wurden Gaskochfeld und Spüle flächenbündig eingeschweißt. Hinter der raumhohen Wandverkleidung, belegt mit roséfarbenem Linoleum, liegt, gut zugänglich, der Vorratsraum.

Some of the fixtures in the house rest on concrete supports that were already built during the shell construction phase. This is also the case with the kitchen counter, which was clad with copper sheeting. The gas hob and sink were welded flush into the textured stainless steel worktop. Behind the floor-to-ceiling wall panelling, covered with rosé-coloured linoleum, is the easily accessible pantry.

Für mich sind Landschaft und Garten ziemlich das Gegenteil eines Hauses. Schon allein aus der Tradition heraus, denn früher hat sich der Mensch Häuser gebaut, um sich vor der Natur beziehungsweise den Naturgewalten, vor wilden Tieren, Kälte und Hitze, zu schützen.
Das Bauwerk entspringt dem menschlichen Tun und dies darf und soll man auch sehen.
Der Garten ist für mich näher an der ursprünglichen Landschaft, und deshalb sind seine Formen auch viel weicher und natürlicher gestaltet. Diese respektvolle Ungleichheit stärkt das Haus und den Garten.

For me, landscape and garden are pretty much the opposite of a house - if only because of tradition, as in the past people built houses to protect themselves from nature or the forces of nature, such as wild animals, cold and heat.
The building is the result of human activity, and this can and should be seen.
In my eyes, the garden is closer to the original landscape, and that's why its forms are much softer and more naturally designed. This respectful disparity strengthens both the house and the garden.

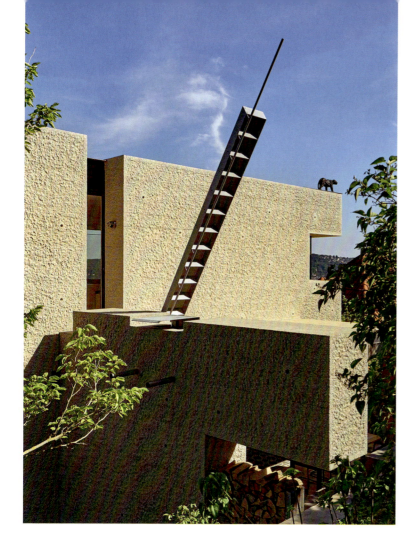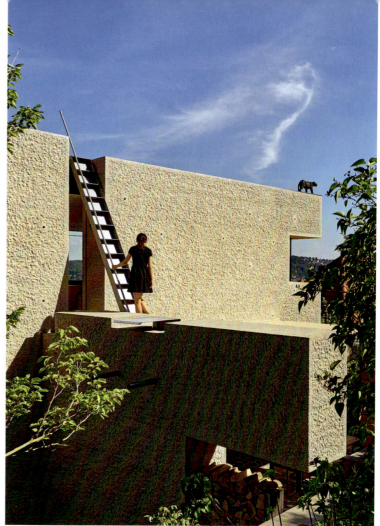

Oberlichte schaffen vielschichtige und lichtdurchflutete Innenräume und die großzügigen, rahmenlosen Verglasungen zur Talseite verwischen die Grenzen zu den vorgelagerten Terrassen.
Auch hier wurden Möbelteile schon im Rohbau betoniert und so entsteht zum Beispiel am Arbeitsplatz eine große Beinfreiheit.

Skylights create multi-layered and light-flooded interiors, and the generous, frameless glazing on the valley side blurs the boundaries to the terraces in front.
Here, too, parts of the furniture were concreted during the shell construction phase, ensuring ample legroom at the workplace, for example.

Während also Teile der Einrichtung und Möblierung sehr stark fixiert sind, sind andere hoch mobil. So wurde das Daybed KAP mit Rädern hinter dem zurückgesetzten Messingsockel versehen, damit es sowohl im Innenraum, als auch als Außenmöbel auf der überdeckten Dachterrasse genutzt werden kann.

While parts of the furnishings are fixed in place, others are extremely mobile.
The KAP daybed, for example, was fitted with wheels behind the recessed brass base so that it can be used both indoors and as outdoor furniture on the sheltered roof terrace.

Zeitlos sind das Feuer, das Essen und das Zusammenkommen – Ein Ort für die kleinen Feste des Lebens.

Fire, food and coming together are timeless – A place for the small celebrations of life.

CROWN HOUSE
HOUSE OF CULTIVATED ELEGANCE, FRANKFURT
2017

Das Grundstück liegt an einer Wohnstraße und ist nach Südwesten zum Tal hin orientiert. Das Baufeld ist etwas tiefer als das Straßenniveau. Das Haus gibt sich deshalb auf der Nordostseite weitgehend geschlossen.
Eine Mauer und die Grünflächen zur Straße hin schützen vor allzu großen Einblicken. Größte Sorgfalt wurde dieser Einfriedung zuteil, denn sie ist auch als eine Art Aufmerksamkeit für den Vorbeigehenden gedacht, der sich an der durchgrünten Zaunanlage, der üppigen Bepflanzung, der vom Steinmetz bearbeiteten Mauer, aber auch am schimmernden Tor erfreuen soll.

Eine Aufweitung des Grundstücks im Norden ermöglichte es, das Garagenbauwerk hier zu platzieren und somit einen Hofraum zu schaffen, der sowohl vor dem Haupteingang, als auch vor dem seitlichen Nebeneingang liegt. Dieser Familieneingang in kurzer Distanz zur Garage erweist sich im täglichen Leben als sehr dienlich.
Hier finden Schuhe, Jacken, Schultaschen und tägliches Allerlei einen Platz, aber auch nach einem Waldspaziergang kann der Hund hier abgeduscht und versorgt werden. Von hier aus sind weitere dienliche Nebenräume, Garderoben und die Wirtschaftsküche auf kurzem Weg erreichbar. Direkt im Anschluss daran liegt die Küche mit dem Essbereich. Von dort gelangt man durch eine großflächige Schiebetür in die eigentliche zentrale Eingangshalle. Auf der gegenüberliegenden Seite ist der Wohnraum mit dem Kamin, an den sich die Bibliothek anschließt.

Eine großzügige Treppe in der Halle erschließt eine Galerie im Obergeschoss, um die herum alle Schlafzimmer und die zugehörigen Bäder angeordnet sind.
Der Elternbereich mit Schlafraum, Ankleide, Bad, Sauna und Arbeitszimmer bildet einen zusammenhängenden, in sich abgeschlossenen Hausteil.
Allen Schlafräumen sind überdachte Terrassen vorgelagert, die einen weiten Blick in die Landschaft bieten.

Ein Gäste-Apartment und ein Sportbereich lagern sich um die Gartenterrasse im Untergeschoss. Des Weiteren sind in diesem Geschoss verschiedene Lager- und Kellerräume, die Haustechnik und ein Weinkeller zu finden.

Das Hauptthema des Hauses ist der Übergang in den Garten, den wir im nahen und mittleren Bereich so gestaltet haben, dass der untere Platz und die neue Pflanzung mit den bestehenden Baumgruppen verschmelzen und eine große Tiefe erzeugen.
Es entsteht das Bild eines weit über das Grundstück hinweg reichenden Landschaftsparks.

The property is located on a residential street and faces southwest towards the valley. The building site is situated slightly below the street level. The house therefore presents itself with almost no openings on the northeast façade.
In addition, a wall and the green spaces along the street prevent too many people from looking in. Great care was taken with this enclosure, because it is also intended as a kind of courtesy for passers-by, who should enjoy the green fencing, the lush greenery and the stonemasonry walls, and also the gleaming gate.

Widening the plot to the north made it possible to place the garage building here and thus create a courtyard that is located in front of both the main and the side entrance. This family entrance at a short distance from the garage proves very useful in day-to-day life.
This is where shoes, jackets, school bags and daily bits and pieces find a place; and the dog can also be given a shower here after a walk in the woods.
From here, other useful ancillary rooms, cloakrooms and the utility kitchen can be reached quickly. Directly adjacent is the kitchen with the dining area, from where a large sliding door leads into the central entrance hall. On the opposite side is the living room with a fireplace and an adjoining library.

A generous staircase in the hall opens onto a gallery on the upper floor, along which all the bedrooms and the associated bathrooms are arranged.
The parents' area with bedroom, dressing room, bathroom, sauna and study forms a coherent, self-contained part of the house.
All bedrooms feature covered terraces, offering expansive views of the landscape.

In the basement, a guest flat and a sports area are laid out around the garden terrace. Furthermore, various storage rooms, the building services and a wine cellar are located on this level.

The main theme of the house is the transition into the garden, the nearby and middle area of which we designed to blend the lower square and the new planting with the existing groups of trees and create a great depth. The result is the impression of a landscape park extending far across the property.

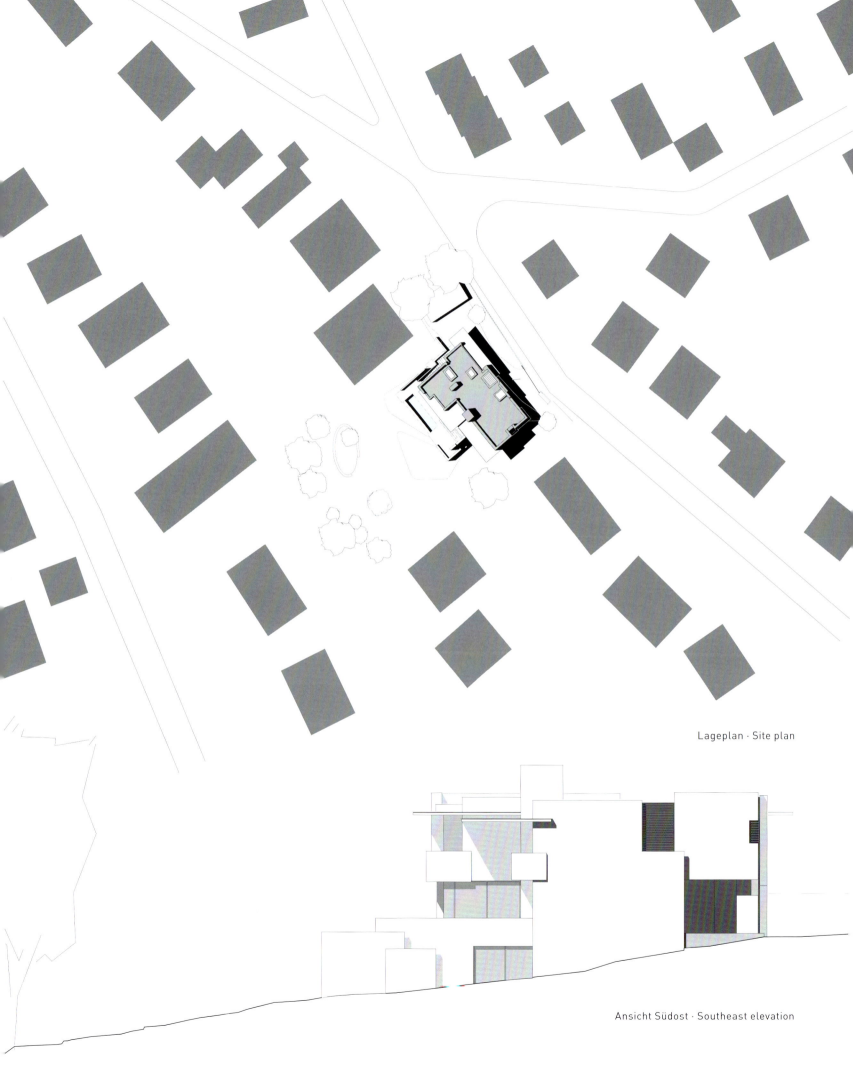

Lageplan · Site plan

Ansicht Südost · Southeast elevation

1	Halle	Hall	
2	Aufzug	Lift	
3	Heimkino	Holodeck	Home theatre	Holodeck
4	Fitness	Fitness	
5	Terrasse	Terrace	
6	Apartment	Apartment	
7	Pooltechnik	Pool plant room	
8	Lager	Storage room	
9	Dusche	Shower	
10	Keller	Cellar	
11	Abstellraum	Storeroom	
12	Umkleide	Changing room	
13	WC	WC	
14	Haustechnik	Building services	
15	Gebäudesteuerung	House automation	
16	Weinkeller	Wine cellar	

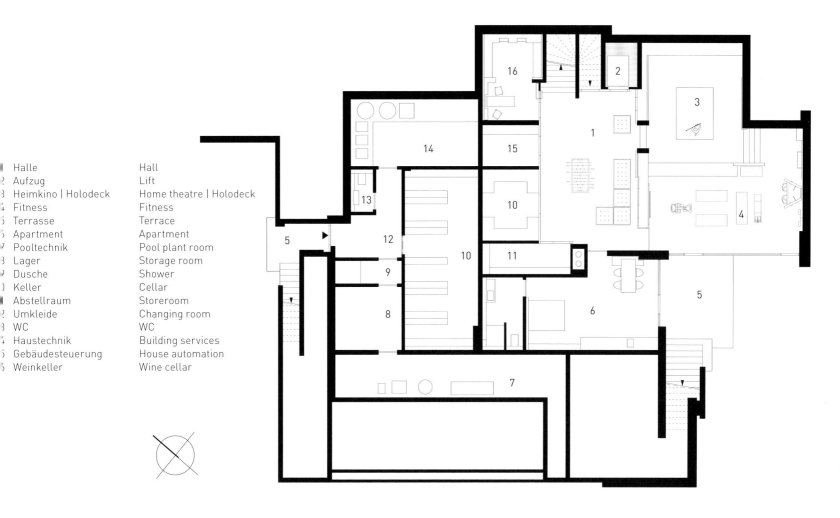

Gartengeschoss · **Level 1** · Garden level

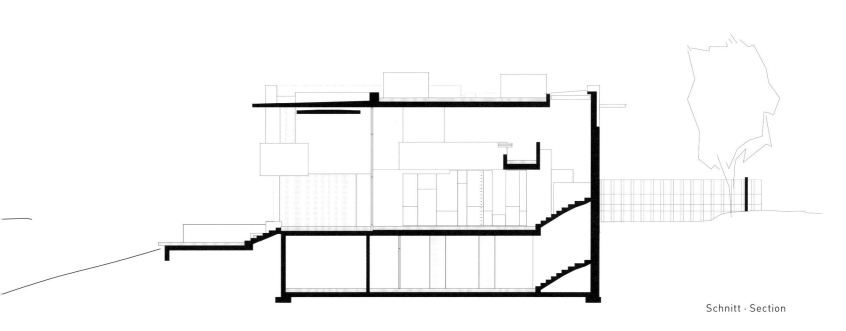

Schnitt · Section

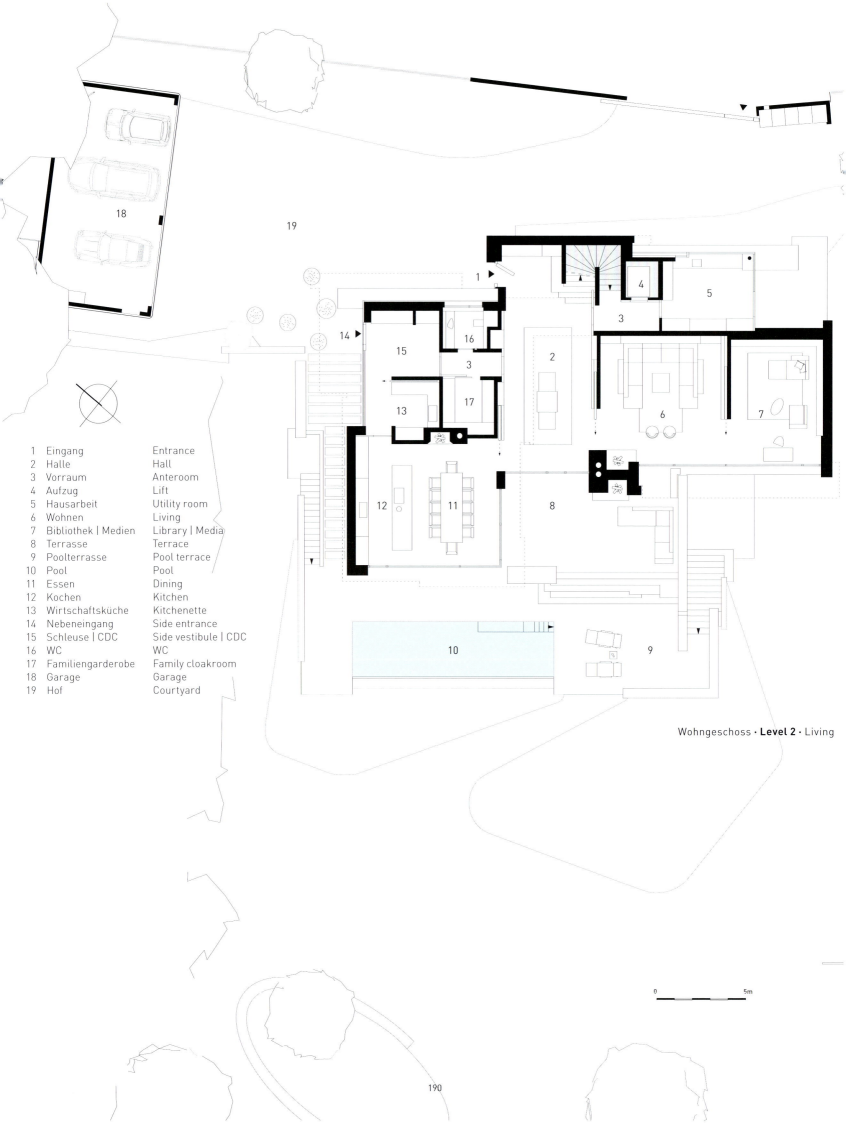

1	Eingang	Entrance
2	Halle	Hall
3	Vorraum	Anteroom
4	Aufzug	Lift
5	Hausarbeit	Utility room
6	Wohnen	Living
7	Bibliothek | Medien	Library | Media
8	Terrasse	Terrace
9	Poolterrasse	Pool terrace
10	Pool	Pool
11	Essen	Dining
12	Kochen	Kitchen
13	Wirtschaftsküche	Kitchenette
14	Nebeneingang	Side entrance
15	Schleuse | CDC	Side vestibule | CDC
16	WC	WC
17	Familiengarderobe	Family cloakroom
18	Garage	Garage
19	Hof	Courtyard

Wohngeschoss · **Level 2** · Living

1	Galerie	Gallery
2	Spielen	Playroom
3	Aufzug	Lift
4	Abstellraum	Utility room
5	Bad	Bathroom
6	Flur	Hallway
7	Loggia	Loggia
8	Kind	Child
9	Schlafen	Master bedroom
10	Elternbad	Master bathroom
11	Ankleide	Dressing room
12	Arbeiten	Studio
13	Sauna	Sauna

Obergeschoss · **Level 3** · Top level

Ansicht Nordwest · Northeast elevation

Die Freiheit der Hand, die Wahrnehmung der Gestalt und das Erleben der Haptik sind uns ein großes Anliegen.
Neben ihrer Solidität und Haltbarkeit ist Bronze ein Material, das durch Witterungseinflüsse, vor allem aber durch den täglichen Gebrauch würdevoll altert und von Tag zu Tag schöner wird.
Ein vom Schmied gefertigter Griff spielt eine leise Melodie in der Hand.

The freedom of the hand, the perception of form and the tactile experience are of great concern to us.
In addition to its solidity and durability, bronze is used here as a material that ages gracefully through the effects of the weather, but above all through daily use, and becomes more beautiful every day.
A handle made by the blacksmith plays a soft melody in one's hand.

Der seitliche Nebeneingang vom Hof ist der Familieneingang, der in einen Schleusenraum führt, der von uns „CDC", abgekürzt für „Camera della Confusione", genannt wird. Dieser Raum ermöglicht die Ablage schmutziger Kleidung, eine Vorreinigung der Schuhe, aber auch das Versorgen des Hundes. Angelieferte Pakete, Schultaschen und tägliches Allerlei finden hier Platz.

Hinterleuchtete Trittplatten aus unbehandeltem Stahl leiten auch in der Dunkelheit zu diesem Nebeneingang. Dass sich darunter auch der eine oder andere notwendige Revisionsschacht verbirgt, wird für Nutzer und Gast zur Nebensache.

The side entrance from the courtyard is the family entrance that leads to a utility room. We call it "CDC", short for "Camera della Confusione". This room is a place where dirty clothes can be taken off, shoes can be pre-cleaned and the dog can be taken care of. Delivered parcels, school bags and daily odds and ends can be stored here.

Backlit stepstones made of untreated steel lead the way to this side entrance, even in the dark. The fact that one or the other necessary inspection shaft is hidden underneath is a minor matter for residents and guests.

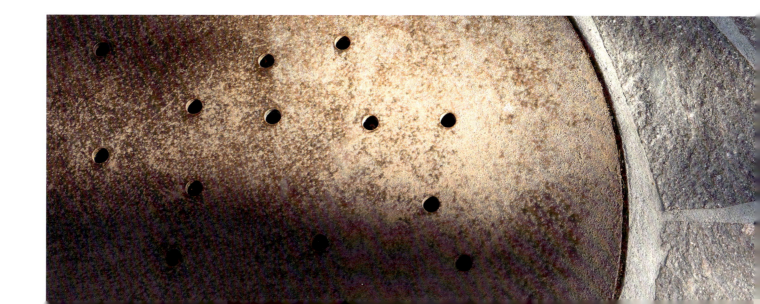

Wie das Zufahrtstor, so ist auch die Garage mit geprägten Edelstahltafeln verkleidet. Durch die Bündigkeit der Tore, die sanft gerundeten Ecken, bildet dieses Schmuckkästchen eine schimmernde Hofwand, die mehr diesem Freiraum dient, als sich auf die dahinterliegende Nutzung zu beziehen.

Like the access gate, the garage is clad in embossed stainless steel plates. Due to the flushness of the gates and the gently rounded corners, this treasure box forms a shimmering courtyard wall that serves this open space more than it relates to the use it conceals.

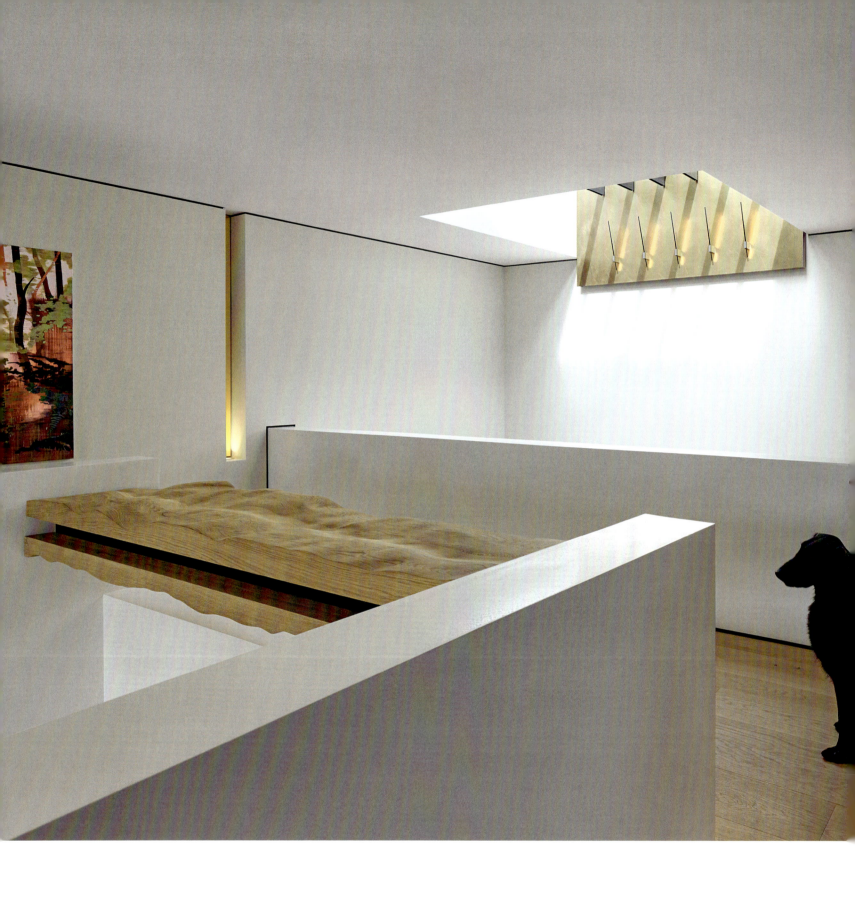

Mit großer Freude und Leidenschaft gestalten wir Küchen und haben hier die Möglichkeit, sie unabhängig von der allgemein üblichen Modulbauweise passend ins Bauwerk einzufügen und als wichtigen Teil des Familienlebens zu integrieren.
Die Kücheninsel ist immer so angeordnet, dass der oder die dort Arbeitende direkten Kontakt zur Familie oder zu den Gästen hat. Darüber hinaus ist hier auch der Überblick in die Halle, zur Hauptterrasse, oder zum Pool und Garten hin gegeben. Es ist die Position einer Schaltzentrale und damit die eigentliche Mitte des Hauses.

Designing kitchens is a great pleasure and a passion for us. Here we have opportunities to integrate them appropriately into the building, independently of the generally usual modular construction method, and make them an integral part of family life.
The kitchen island is always positioned so that the person working at it is in direct contact with the family or guests. Moreover, it offers an overview of the hall, the main terrace and a view of the pool and garden. It is the position of a control centre and thus the actual heart of the house.

Der Wechsel des Lichts, aber auch der jahreszeitliche Wandel des Gartens mit seinen unterschiedlichen Blütenständen begleiten den architektonischen Ort über die Zeit.
Das Haus feiert die Beständigkeit und erscheint doch in immer neuem Gewand.
Im Sommer steht es über einem verschwenderischen Blütenmeer, doch leider sind die meisten unserer Aufnahmen erst im Spätsommer, nach dem Rückschnitt des Lavendels, entstanden.

The change of light, but also the seasonal change of the garden with its different inflorescences accompany the architectural space over time.
The house celebrates permanence and yet always appears in a new guise.
In summer, the house overlooks a lavish sea of blossoms. Unfortunately, most of our photos were taken in late summer, when the lavender had already been pruned back.

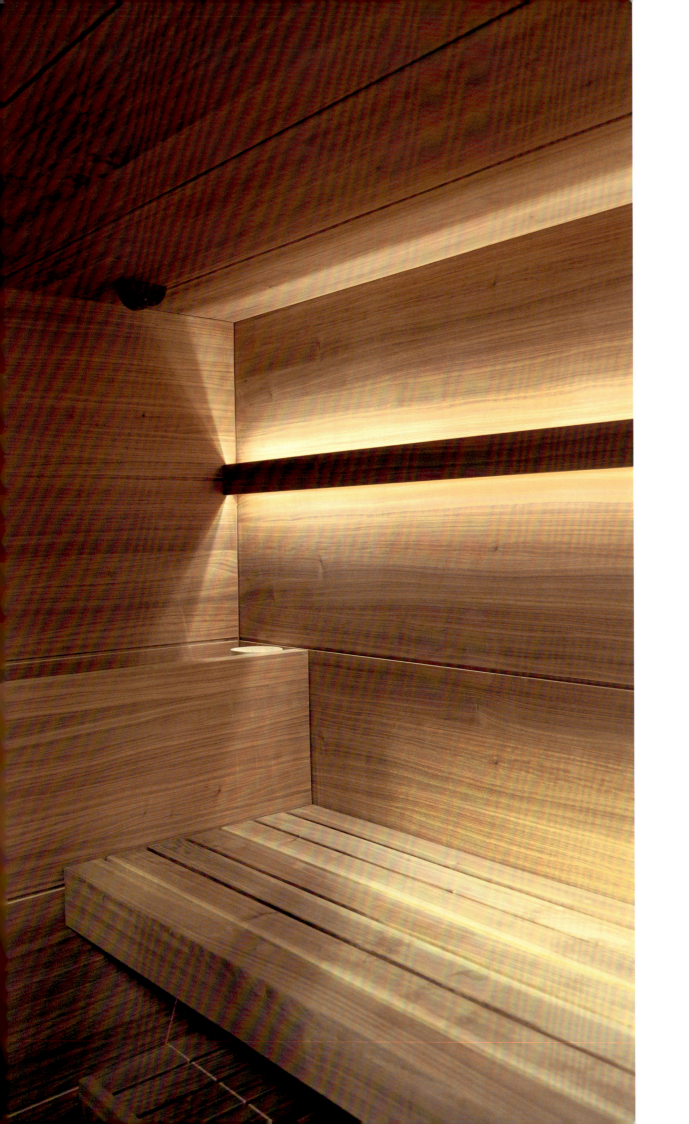

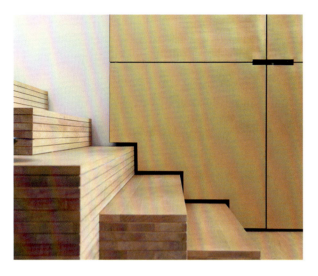

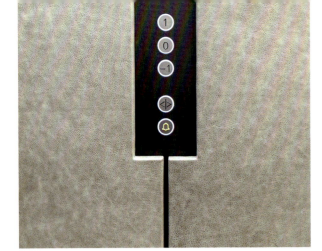

Im Sinne des Gesamtwerks entwerfen wir alle Einbauten, Möbel und Gegenstände des Alltags und integrieren die Technik, erfinden aber auch Beschläge und Konstruktionen, die nicht auf dem Markt erhältlich sind.

So sind uns Schiebetüren, die weder einer Schiene an der Decke, noch einer Führung am Boden bedürfen, so wichtig gewesen, dass wir diese entwickelten. Nichts stört so den Fluss des Raumes.

Auch für Backöfen und Küchengeräte konstruierten wir einen senkrechten Hubbeschlag, so dass der Raum auf die wechselnde gestalterische Qualität dieser Geräte nicht angewiesen ist. Alle Oberflächen werden in Materialien ausgeführt, die fest, langlebig und in hohem Maße alterungsfähig sind, oder am besten durch ihren Gebrauch über die Jahre schöner werden. Wir sind dankbar, dass wir unter der Handwerkerschaft engagierte Mitstreiter gefunden haben, die unseren unbedingten Willen zur Qualität mit uns teilen.

In keeping with the overall project, we design all fixtures, furniture and everyday objects and integrate the technical installations, but we also develop fittings, hardware and constructions that are not available on the market.
Sliding doors, for example, which require neither a guiding rail on the ceiling nor on the floor, were so important to us that we developed them ourselves. So nothing disturbs the flowing space.
We also designed a vertical lifting fitting for ovens and kitchen appliances, so that the room is not dependent on the changing design quality of these devices. All surfaces are made of materials that are solid, durable and will age gracefully, or ideally become more beautiful through their use over the years. We are grateful that we have found committed comrades-in-arms among the craftsmen who share with us our unconditional commitment to quality.

HAUS AM WALD
PRIVATE RESIDENCE, STUTTGART
2016

Das Grundstück befindet sich am Ende einer Sackgasse am nördlichen Rand eines Stadtteils von Stuttgart und liegt unmittelbar am Wald.
Die Garage und die anschließende Brüstung grenzen Haus und Garten zur Straße hin ab.
Eine raumbegrenzende Wand, in die das Garagentor unsichtbar integriert ist, leitet den Ankommenden zum Hauseingang.

Der Zugang führt in eine Halle mit einer 7 Meter langen Garderobenwand. Ein großer Luftraum über der Halle verbindet alle drei Geschosse des Hauses und sorgt für vielfältige Blickbeziehungen.
Über diesen Luftraum mit drei quadratischen Oberlichtern wird die im untersten Geschoss liegende Halle mit Licht geflutet. In den dreigeschossigen Raum könnte bei Bedarf leicht ein Aufzug eingebaut werden.
Im Untergeschoss sind neben der Garderobe Lagerflächen, ein Weinkeller, sowie ein Sauna- und Fitnessbereich untergebracht; hier befinden sich auch die Technik- und Serviceräume.
Der Ess- und Wohnbereich im Erdgeschoss präsentiert sich als großzügig fließendes Raumkontinuum und orientiert sich mit seiner raumhohen Verglasung über die Terrasse hinweg in Richtung Westen zum Garten, zum Pool und zum Wald hin.
Alle anderen Verglasungen in diesem Geschoss sind so angeordnet, dass die jeweilige Nachbarbebauung ausgeblendet wird.

Über eine Treppe an der nordöstlichen Ecke des Hauses erreicht man das Obergeschoss mit den privaten Räumen der dreiköpfigen Familie.
Auf der Galerie zum Luftraum hin ist ein großer Schreibplatz, dahinter ein geschlossenes Arbeitszimmer für ein ruhigeres Arbeiten.
Das Haus wurde mit Porenbetonaußenwänden in Stärken zwischen 50 und 65 Zentimetern ausgeführt. Dadurch und dank einer Photovoltaikanlage, die eine Luft-Wärmepumpe versorgt, erreicht das Haus eine herausragende Energieeffizienz.

Durch die Lage des Gartens oberhalb der Garagen entsteht zwischen Wald und Gebäude ein uneinsichtiger, geschützter Raum, gleich einer Lichtung im Wald.
Das Haus ist mehr Ort in der Landschaft, als es sich auf die heterogene Umgebungsbebauung bezieht.

The property is located at the end of a cul-de-sac on the northern edge of a district of Stuttgart and directly adjoining a forest.
The garage volume and the adjacent parapet separate the house and garden from the street.
A space-defining wall, which invisibly integrates the garage gate, guides those arriving to the entrance of the house.

The entrance leads directly into a hall with a 7-metre long wall of built-in wardrobes. A large void above the entrance hall connects all three levels of the building and provides for a variety of visual connections.
This void with its numerous skylights allows the hall on the lowest level to be flooded with daylight. A lift can easily be installed in the three-storey space at a later date.

Besides the cloakroom and storage areas, downstairs also accommodates a wine cellar, a sauna and fitness area, as well as the technical and utility rooms.
The dining and living area on the level above is designed as a generous spatial continuum, with its floor-to-ceiling glazing facing west across the terrace and towards the garden, the pool and the forest.
All other glazing on this level is arranged so that the neighbouring buildings are out of view.

A staircase in the north-eastern corner leads to the top floor accommodating the private rooms for the family of three.
A large desk facing the void is placed on the gallery, and behind it is a separate study for more focused work.

Thanks to its external walls made of aerated concrete with thicknesses ranging from 50 to 65 cm, a photovoltaic system and an air-source heat pump supplied by it, the house achieves an outstanding level of energy efficiency.

The layout of the garden above the garages creates a protected space hidden from view between the forest and the building, resembling a forest clearing.
The house is a place in the landscape rather than relating to the heterogeneous buildings surrounding it.

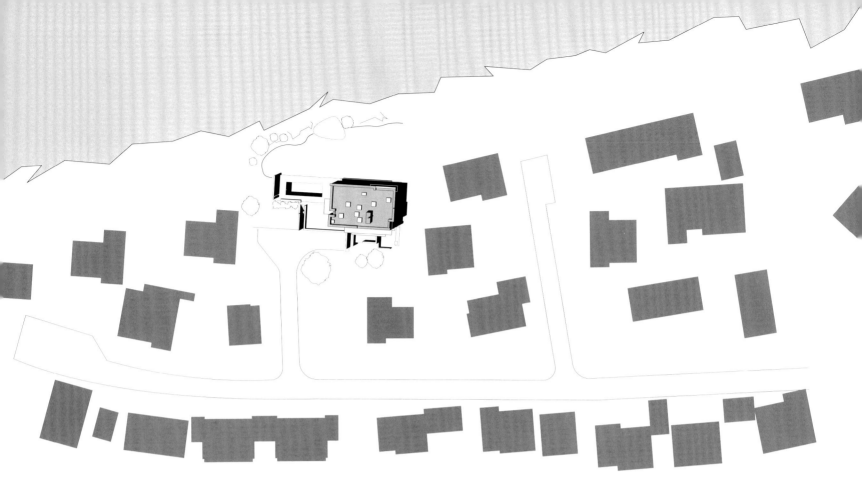

Lageplan · Site plan

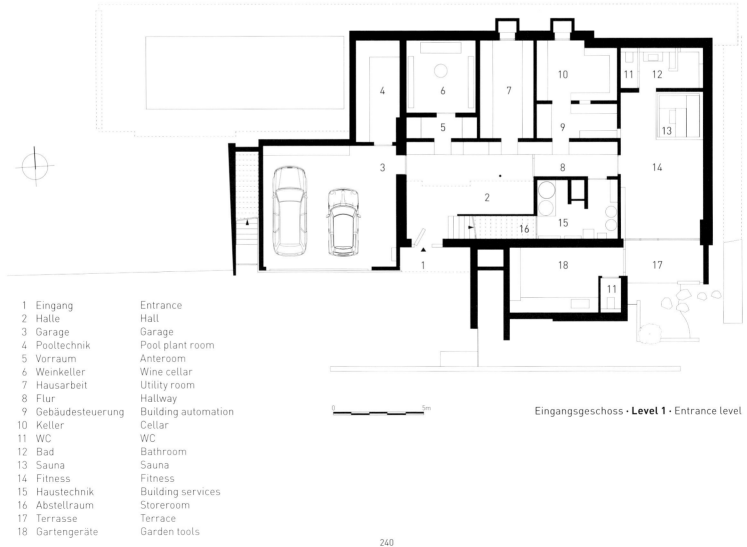

1 Eingang — Entrance
2 Halle — Hall
3 Garage — Garage
4 Pooltechnik — Pool plant room
5 Vorraum — Anteroom
6 Weinkeller — Wine cellar
7 Hausarbeit — Utility room
8 Flur — Hallway
9 Gebäudesteuerung — Building automation
10 Keller — Cellar
11 WC — WC
12 Bad — Bathroom
13 Sauna — Sauna
14 Fitness — Fitness
15 Haustechnik — Building services
16 Abstellraum — Storeroom
17 Terrasse — Terrace
18 Gartengeräte — Garden tools

Eingangsgeschoss · **Level 1** · Entrance level

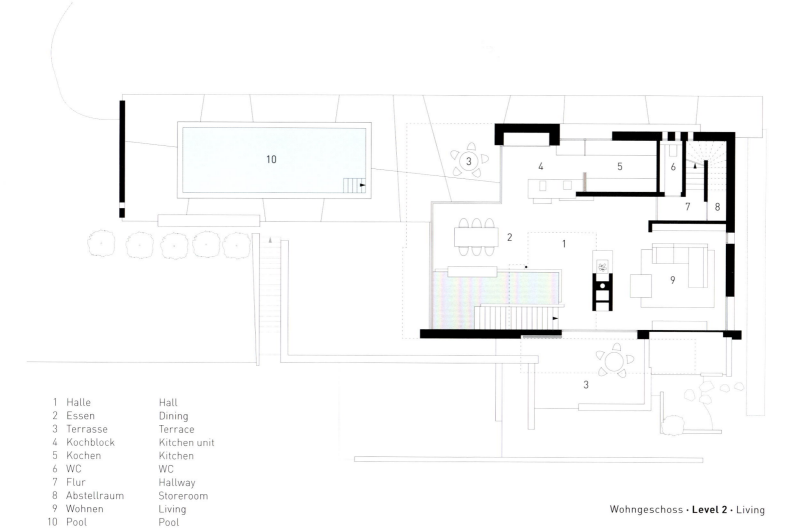

1 Halle — Hall
2 Essen — Dining
3 Terrasse — Terrace
4 Kochblock — Kitchen unit
5 Kochen — Kitchen
6 WC — WC
7 Flur — Hallway
8 Abstellraum — Storeroom
9 Wohnen — Living
10 Pool — Pool

Wohngeschoss · **Level 2** · Living

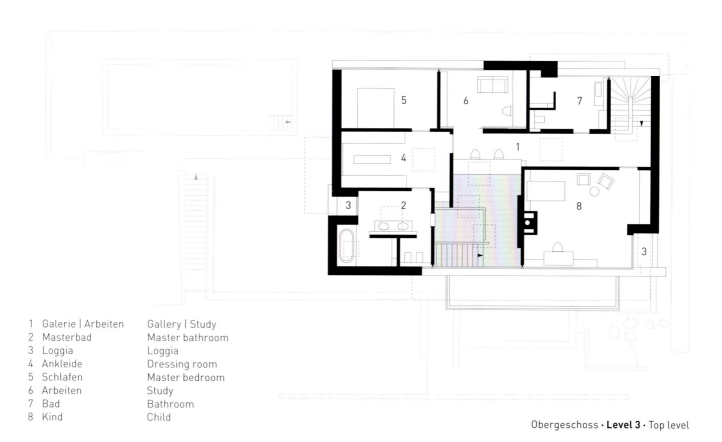

1 Galerie | Arbeiten — Gallery | Study
2 Masterbad — Master bathroom
3 Loggia — Loggia
4 Ankleide — Dressing room
5 Schlafen — Master bedroom
6 Arbeiten — Study
7 Bad — Bathroom
8 Kind — Child

Obergeschoss · **Level 3** · Top level

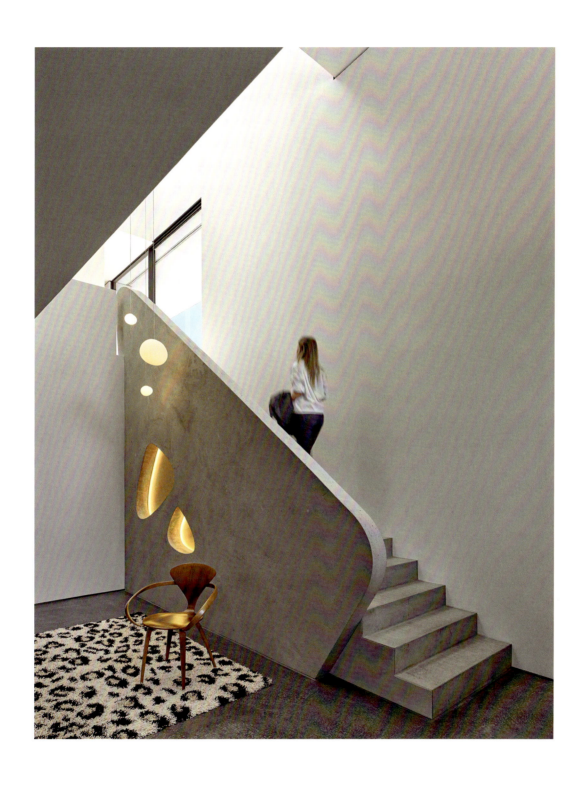

Ein Luftraum über alle drei Ebenen belichtet auch das tiefliegende Eingangsgeschoß.
Er erzeugt Offenheit und Transparenz, ist aber auch gleichzeitig Raum für den im Bedarfsfall zu ergänzenden Aufzug.

A void extending across all three floors also floods the low-lying entrance level with daylight.
It creates openness and transparency, while simultaneously providing space for the lift, which can be installed if the need arises.

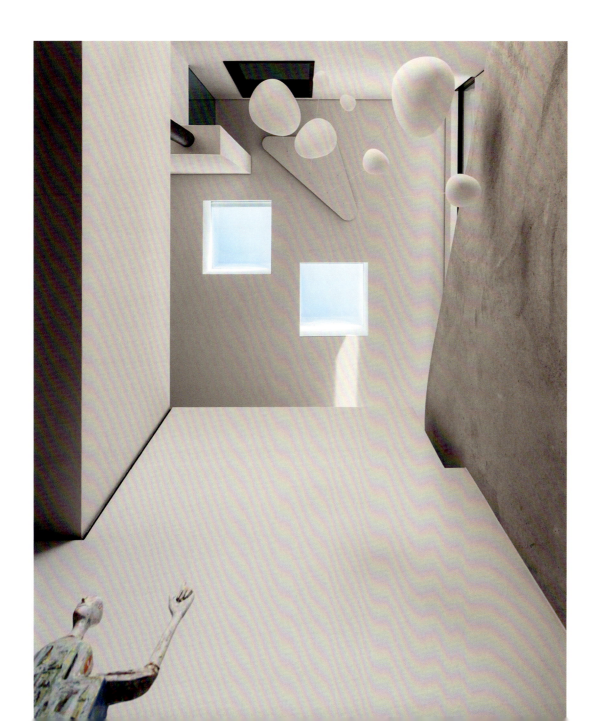

Wenn ich an die damals erarbeiteten Bilder einer Waldlichtung denke und mich an die damit einhergehende räumliche Stimmung zwischen geschlossen und offen, zwischen Licht und Schatten erinnere, dann ist hier heute der Rücken frei und beschützt, und ich blicke mit Leichtigkeit zu diesem besonderen Ort.

When I think of the images of a forest clearing elaborated at that time and the spatial mood between closed and open, between light and shadow associated with it, then one's back is covered and protected here, and I look with ease at this special place.

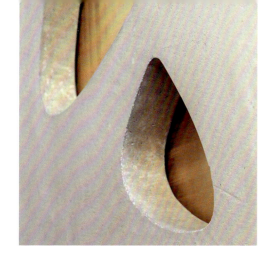

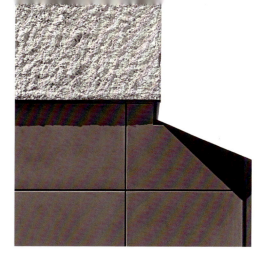

Wie bei allen unseren Projekten gibt es auch bei diesem Haus experimentelle Anteile.
So wurden hier die schon jahrelang, vor allem als Gartenwände erforschten, gespitzten Betonoberflächen nochmals großflächig in verschiedenen Bewitterungssituationen eingesetzt, bevor wir sie dann bei nachfolgenden Projekten für die ganze Gebäudehülle verwendet haben.

As with all our projects, there are also experimental elements to this house.
For example, the chiselled concrete surfaces that had already been researched for years, especially as garden walls, were used again extensively in various weathering situations before we then adopted them for the entire building envelope in subsequent projects.

ROTTMANN HOUSE
PRIVATE RESIDENCE, WIESBADEN
2015

Das Grundstück liegt im Inneren eines Wohnquartiers oberhalb der Burgruine Sonnenberg mit Blick auf die gegenüberliegenden, bewaldeten Hänge. Über eine Stichstraße wird das Grundstück erschlossen. Ein geschwungener Weg leitet den Ankommenden über einen Vorplatz vorbei an der Garage zum Hauseingang.

Ein großer Luftraum über dem Eingangsbereich verbindet alle drei Geschosse des Hauses miteinander und sorgt für vielfältige Blickbeziehungen. Belichtet wird dieser Raum über eine große Glasfläche im Norden und ein Oberlicht, durch das zu jeder Tageszeit ein Sonnenstrahl bis tief ins Haus fällt.

Im Gartengeschoss sind Zugang, Lager, Technik- und Nebenflächen, aber auch Büro- und Gästeräume.
Eine skulpturale Treppe hinter einer raumgliedernden Wandscheibe führt entlang einer Sichtbetonwand ins Erdgeschoss. Durch das lageweise Einbringen eines Einkornbetons unter Verwendung von hellem und dunklem Zuschlag entstand ein Zebramuster, das über drei Geschosse bis unter das Oberlicht reicht.

Das Erdgeschoss ist ein offenes Raumkontinuum, dessen überwiegend raumhohe Verglasung sich Richtung Süden und Westen über den Garten und das Tal orientiert. Von der offenen Halle gelangt man in den Wohnbereich mit Kamin, sowie in den Essbereich und die Küche, an die sich im Süden die Terrasse und der Pool anschließen. Durch eine integrierte Tür in der Küchenrückwand gelangt man zur Wirtschaftsküche.

Im Obergeschoss liegen die privaten Räume der vierköpfigen Familie mit vorgelagerten Balkonen und Loggien.
Genauso wichtig wie eine zeitgemäße Technik und Energieversorgung waren der Bauherrschaft Einfachheit, Zeitlosigkeit und hohe Qualität und die Verarbeitung von dauerhaften, ehrlichen und echten Materialien.
Das gesamte Gebäude wurde mit Porenbetonaußenwänden in Stärken zwischen 50 und 65 Zentimetern ausgeführt. Als Außenputz wurde ein mineralischer Dickputz eingesetzt und das Haus sowohl innen, als auch außen mit mineralischen Anstrichen versehen.
Das Haus wird mittels Geothermie erwärmt, der Pool mit einer Luft-Wärmepumpe, die erforderliche Elektrizität liefert eine großflächige Photovoltaik-Anlage.

The property is located at the heart of a residential neighbourhood above the ruins of Sonnenberg Castle with a view of the wooded slopes on the opposite side. The property is accessed via a cul-de-sac. A curved pathway leads those arriving across a forecourt and past the garage to the entrance of the house.

A large void above the entrance area connects all three floors and provides a variety of visual connections. This space is naturally lit by a large glazed area in the north and a skylight, through which sunlight reaches deep into the house at all times of the day.

The entrance is located on the garden level, as are storage rooms, technical and ancillary areas, a home office and a guest room.
A sculptural staircase located behind a space-structuring wall slab leads along a exposed concrete wall to the main living area upstairs. By layering a single-grain concrete with light and dark aggregates, a zebra pattern was created that extends over three storeys right up to the skylight.

The living level is designed as an open-plan spatial continuum with predominantly floor-to-ceiling glazing facing south and west over the garden and valley. The open hall leads to the living area with fireplace and to the dining area and the kitchen, which is adjoined by a terrace and a pool facing south. An integrated door in the kitchen back wall provides access to a kitchenette.

The private rooms with balconies and loggias for the family of four are located on the top floor.
The client considered simplicity, timelessness and high quality and the use of durable, authentic and genuine materials to be just as important as latest technologies and responsible energy supply.
The entire building was constructed with exterior walls made of aerated concrete with thicknesses between 50 and 65 cm. A thick layer of mineral plaster was applied on the outside, and the house was painted with mineral paints both inside and out.
The house is heated using geothermal energy, the pool with an air-source heat pump, and the required electricity is supplied by a large-scale photovoltaic system.

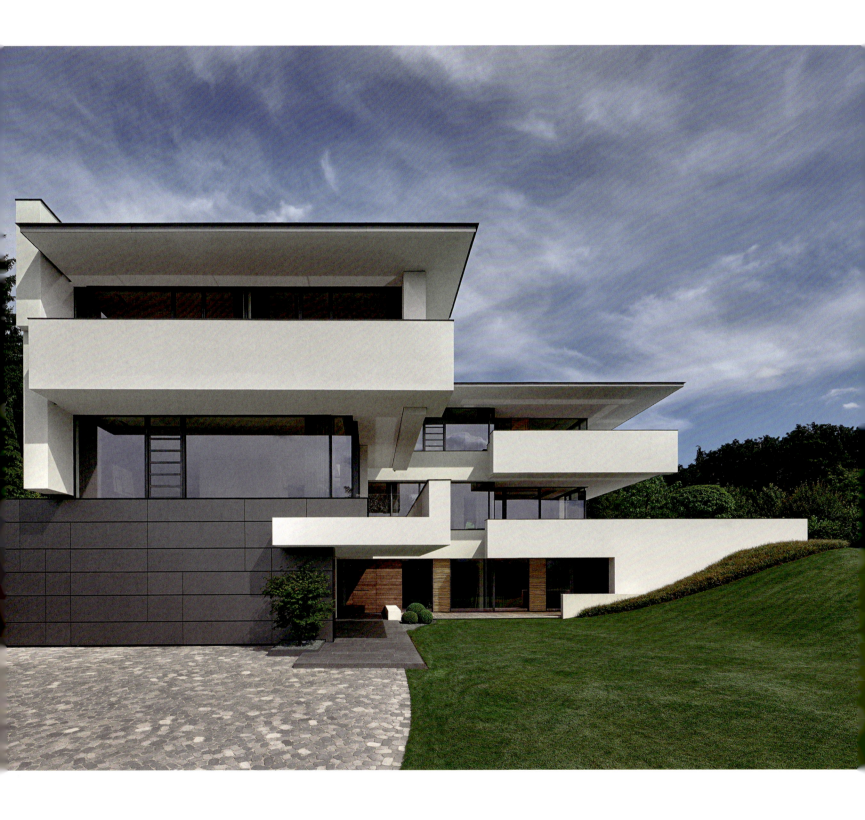

Lageplan · Site plan

3D Schnitt · 3D section

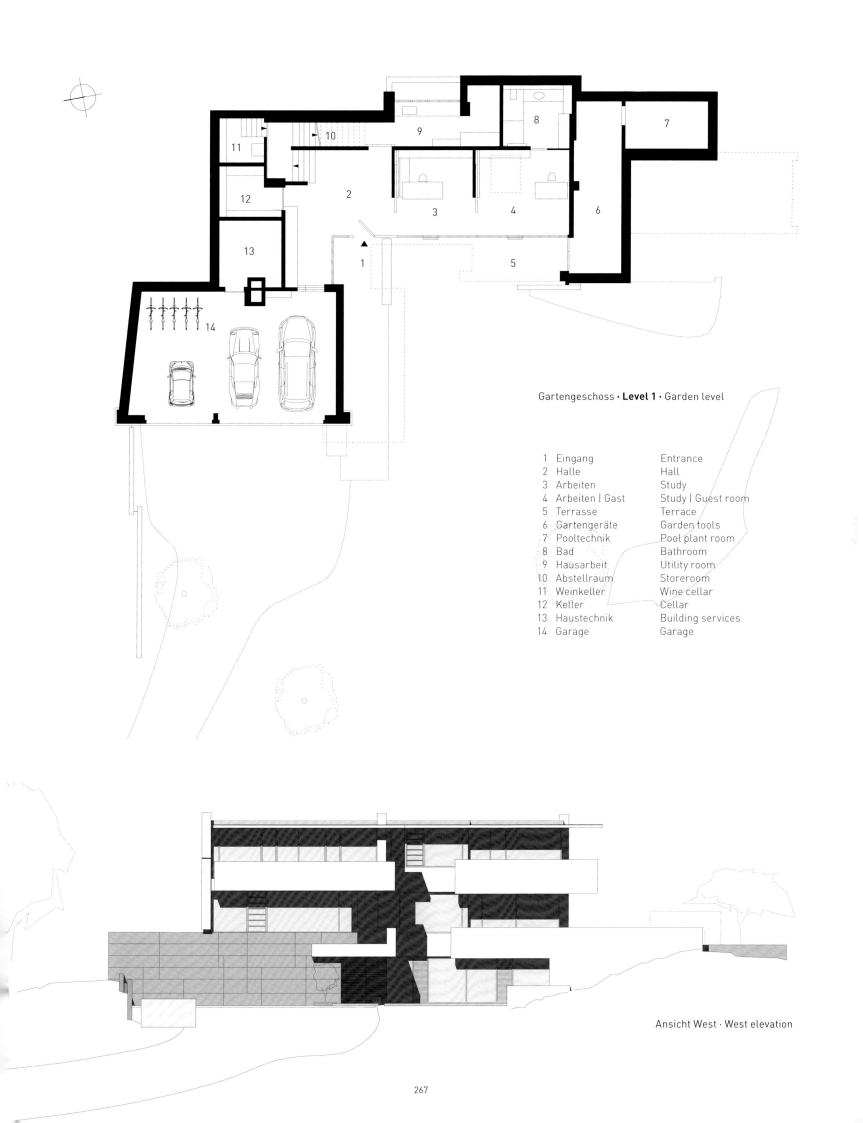

Gartengeschoss · **Level 1** · Garden level

1 Eingang — Entrance
2 Halle — Hall
3 Arbeiten — Study
4 Arbeiten | Gast — Study | Guest room
5 Terrasse — Terrace
6 Gartengeräte — Garden tools
7 Pooltechnik — Pool plant room
8 Bad — Bathroom
9 Hausarbeit — Utility room
10 Abstellraum — Storeroom
11 Weinkeller — Wine cellar
12 Keller — Cellar
13 Haustechnik — Building services
14 Garage — Garage

Ansicht West · West elevation

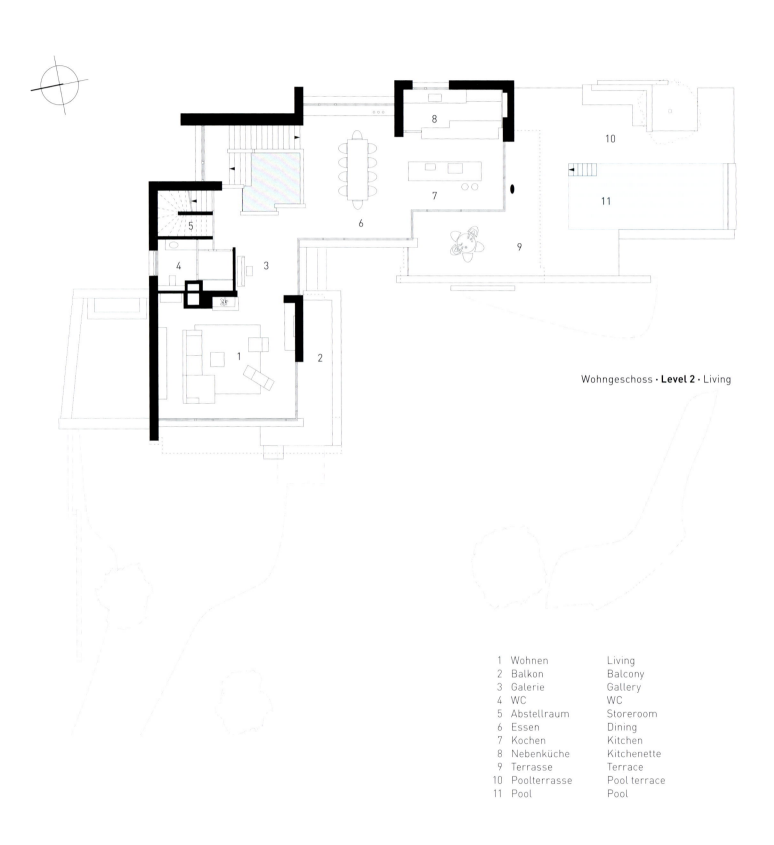

Wohngeschoss · **Level 2** · Living

1 Wohnen — Living
2 Balkon — Balcony
3 Galerie — Gallery
4 WC — WC
5 Abstellraum — Storeroom
6 Essen — Dining
7 Kochen — Kitchen
8 Nebenküche — Kitchenette
9 Terrasse — Terrace
10 Poolterrasse — Pool terrace
11 Pool — Pool

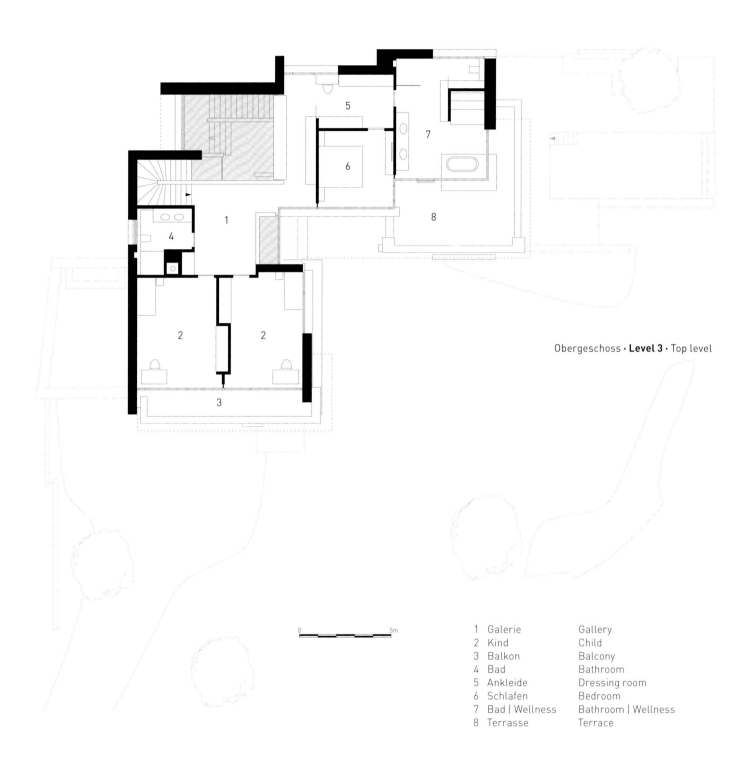

Obergeschoss · **Level 3** · Top level

1 Galerie — Gallery
2 Kind — Child
3 Balkon — Balcony
4 Bad — Bathroom
5 Ankleide — Dressing room
6 Schlafen — Bedroom
7 Bad | Wellness — Bathroom | Wellness
8 Terrasse — Terrace

Durch das lageweise Einbringen eines Einkornbetons unter Verwendung von hellem und dunklem Zuschlag entstand ein Zebramuster, das über drei Geschosse bis unter das Oberlicht reicht und auch für eine hohe Schallabsorption in der offenen Halle sorgt.

By layering a single-grain concrete with light and dark aggregates, a zebra pattern was created that extends over three storeys right up to the skylight and also ensures high sound absorption in the open hall.

Kunst ist Schönheit und damit eine Offenbarung. Ihr soll man sich nicht verschließen um eines Tages feststellen zu können, dass die höchste Kunst die Kunst des Lebens ist.

Art is beauty and thus a revelation. One should not deprive oneself of it in order to be able to realise one day that the supreme art is the art of living.

DIE SEHNSUCHT NACH DEM GESAMTWERK

ALEXANDER BRENNER

Vielfalt und Offenheit für andere Denkweisen, aber auch das Bewusstsein für unsere Wurzeln von Athen über Rom, die Renaissance und die Aufklärung, bis hin zur Moderne prägen unsere Arbeit.

Immer beherrscht uns der Wunsch, alles bis ins Kleinste richtig zu machen. Das führt uns dazu, alle Projekte mit derselben Intensität und demselben Enthusiasmus zu bearbeiten. Ob es sich dabei um einen Stadtteil oder um ein Sideboard für eines unserer Gebäude handelt, spielt dabei keine Rolle.

Nun sind es beim Erscheinen dieses dritten Bandes schon beinahe 33 Jahre, in denen wir so denken und arbeiten. Ich blicke auf eine aufregende und spannende Zeit zurück, in der wir täglich für das Schöne gekämpft haben. Niemals hat die Leidenschaft, mit der wir uns um das Ganze oder eine Einzelheit bemüht haben, nachgelassen. Und darauf, dass wir immer für die Sache gebrannt haben, bin ich heute auch ein wenig stolz.

Natürlich gab es auch Tage, an denen uns weniger gute Nachrichten zu einzelnen Projekten erreicht haben, aber ich kann mich an keinen einzigen Tag erinnern, an dem ich nicht entweder mit Freude ins Atelier oder mit großer Freude aus dem Atelier gegangen bin.

An unserer Grundhaltung und unseren Zielen hat sich wenig geändert, aber außerhalb unserer kleinen Insel hat sich die Welt kräftig verändert.

Die Vorstellung, dass das Bauen als eine Art Mine zur Gewinnung von Geldscheinen betrachtet wird, hat weiter zugenommen. Es gibt immer weniger verantwortungsvolle Bauherrschaften, die die gesellschaftliche Relevanz des Bauens ernst nehmen, denn immer mehr, vor allem große Bauvorhaben, werden auf der Grundlage von Renditeberechnungen durch Investorengruppen veranlasst.

So wird heute der Bauunterhalt teilweise schon den Mietern übertragen, was einem kontinuierlichen Abbruch gleichkommt. Nach 20 Jahren soll sich ein Bauwerk rentiert haben, und die Zeit danach bleibt ungewiss. Es klingt wie Hohn, wenn dabei auch noch von Nachhaltigkeit gesprochen wird.

Andererseits beginnen viele Menschen inzwischen zu verstehen, dass sich Nachhaltigkeit nicht nur in Rechenwerten und Dämmstärken zeigt. Ich beobachte von vielen Seiten ein gesteigertes Interesse an der Haltung, die wir sie schon seit Anbeginn vertreten. Bei vielen gibt es inzwischen ein großes Unbehagen gegenüber kurzlebigen, auf raschen Ersatz ausgelegten Produkten. Weltweit werden deshalb Kreislaufthemen wie Cradle to Cradle diskutiert und speziell beim Bauen schon der spätere Rückbau geplant. Wie in anderen gesellschaftlichen Bereichen, zum

THE LONGING FOR THE TOTAL WORK OF ART

ALEXANDER BRENNER

Diversity and openness to other ways of thinking, but also an awareness of our roots – extending from Athens to Rome, the Renaissance and the Enlightenment, all the way to the modern age – shape our work.

We always aspire to get everything right, down to the smallest detail. This makes us work with the same intensity and enthusiasm on all of our projects, regardless of whether it's a complete neighbourhood or a sideboard for one of our projects.

Now, at the time of the publication of this third volume, it is almost 33 years that we have been acting and working this way. I look back on exciting and thrilling years in which we have fought for beauty each and every day. There has never been a time when the passion we devote to the whole or to a detail has diminished. I am actually a little proud of the fact that we have always been fervently committed to the cause.

Of course, there were days when we received less positive news about individual projects, but I can't remember a single day when I was not either glad to go into the studio or very happy when I left it.

Little has changed in our basic attitude and our goals, but outside our little island, the world has continued to change vigorously.

The notion that building is a kind of mine for extracting money seems to be even more widespread. The number of responsible clients who take the social relevance of building seriously is decreasing as more and more building projects, especially large ones, are being commissioned on the basis of return calculations by investor groups.

Today, for example, some of the building maintenance is already being transferred to the tenants, which is tantamount to continuous demolition. After 20 years, the building is supposed to have paid off and the time after that remains uncertain. It is almost a mockery that sustainability is being mentioned in this context.

On the other hand, I believe that many people are now beginning to understand that sustainability does not only qualify in terms of calculated values and insulation thicknesses. Actually, I observe a generally increased interest in the approach we have been advocating since the very beginning. I also believe that many people are now very uneasy about non-durable products that are designed for early replacement. That is why topics such as cradle-to-cradle are being discussed all around the world, and later deconstruction is already being planned, especially in the building sector. As in other areas of society, for example concerning food, a greater awareness of how things are produced and marketed is gradually emerg-

Beispiel beim Essen, entsteht allmählich ein größeres Bewusstsein gegenüber dem, wie etwas produziert und vermarktet wird. Deshalb stehen heute auch Fragen zur Baubiologie und Wohngesundheit immer mehr im Fokus. Wir glauben deshalb, mit unseren Konstruktionen und den gewählten Materialien auch weiterhin auf dem richtigen Weg zu sein und dies in allen Belangen des Hauses. So konstruieren wir Wandaufbauten, ohne dass dabei zusätzliche, womöglich mineralölbasierte, Dämmstoffe erforderlich werden. Auch bei Zwischen- oder Trittschalldämmungen experimentieren wir mit alternativen Materialien und so wurden beispielsweise beim Brenner Research House Holzfaserplatten zwischen Rohdecke und Estrich verlegt.

Auch die thermische Bauteilaktivierung erscheint uns als sehr sinnfällig, zumal bei unseren Bauten keine abgehängten Zwischendecken zum Einsatz kommen. Trenn- und Zwischenwände bauen wir gegen jeden Trend weiterhin aus massiven Kalksandsteinen hoher Dichte, was neben einem guten Schallschutz zu einer hohen Speichermasse und damit einem ausgewogenen Temperatur- und Feuchtehaushalt führt. Das Verputzen der Innenflächen mit Kalkputz trägt zu einem ausgeglichenen Raumklima bei.

Die Einbauten, Möbel sowie unsere Küchen, werden aus Massivholz gefertigt und mit baubiologisch unbedenklichen Oberflächen, wie zum Beispiel Linoleum, belegt. Viele Materialien werden aber auch gänzlich unversiegelt und unbehandelt eingesetzt, oder lediglich mit etwas Leinöl eingelassen.

Die Kontrolle über all diese verwendeten Materialien ist uns gegeben, da wir sämtliche Einbauten entwerfen und konstruieren und diese dann handwerklich gefertigt werden. So bleibt der Anteil an Serienprodukten denkbar gering.

Produkte und Ausstattungsgegenstände, die wir nicht fertigen lassen, werden mit den gleichen Kriterien geprüft, vor allem auch auf ihre Dauerhaftigkeit, ihre Funktionalität und ihre sorgfältige Gestaltung. Wir vermeiden alles Modische und legen größten Wert auf die Zeitlosigkeit der eingesetzten Produkte.

Wir fühlen uns nicht nur während des Entstehungszeitpunkts für unsere Häuser verantwortlich, sondern auch dafür, wie sie noch nach vielen Jahren erscheinen werden. Deshalb gilt unser tägliches Streben dem gut Gestalteten wie dem gut Gemachten.

Diese Grundhaltung hat sich in den letzten Jahren nicht verändert und deshalb werden dem Leser des zuvor erschienenen Band 2 (2010–2015) die folgenden Zeilen sehr bekannt vorkommen.

ing. That is why the focus is increasingly shifting towards building biology and healthy living.

We therefore believe that we are still on the right track with our constructions and our way of using materials – in all aspects of the house. For example, we design wall structures without the need for additional, possibly mineral oil-based, insulation materials. We also experiment with alternative materials for intermediate or impact sound insulation. In the Brenner Research House, for example, wood fibre boards were laid between the raw floor slab and the screed flooring.

We also consider component activation a very sensible option, especially since no suspended false ceilings are used in our buildings. Against all trends, we continue to build partition and interior walls from solid, high-density sand-lime bricks, which, in addition to good sound insulation, provides a large storage mass and thus a balanced temperature and humidity level. Rendering the interior surfaces with lime plaster contributes to a well-balanced indoor climate.

Built-in elements, furniture and kitchen units are made of solid wood and finished with biologically safe surfaces, such as linoleum. However, many materials are also used completely unsealed and untreated, or are simply finished with linseed oil.

We have control over all the materials used, as we design and construct all the fixtures and fittings, which are then handcrafted. Hence, we keep the proportion of mass-produced products to a minimum.

Products and furnishings that we do not have manufactured are tested according to the same criteria, especially with regard to their durability, functionality and careful design. We avoid anything fashionable and attach utmost importance to the timelessness of the products selected.

Viele Entwicklungen wurden nur dadurch möglich, dass auch die Ausführenden bereit waren, neue Wege zu beschreiten, Risiken einzugehen und sich mit uns oft auch weit außerhalb der gängigen Normen zu bewegen. Ich bin unendlich dankbar, dass wir eine ganze Reihe von solch tapferen und engagierten Mitstreitern gefunden haben. Mit vielen von ihnen arbeiten wir heute noch zusammen. Dass auch diese Handwerker unsere Architektur, unsere Art des Umgangs und die Art der Zusammenarbeit schätzen, erweist sich auch dadurch, dass wir für viele von ihnen das eigene Wohnhaus geplant haben; zuletzt das **Haus im Weinberg** für einen der beiden Eigentümer unserer Rohbaufirma.

We feel responsible not only for the moment when our houses are built, but also for their appearance many years later. That is why our daily striving is aimed at good design and also at good craftsmanship.

This basic attitude has not changed in recent years, and therefore the following lines will sound very familiar to the reader of the previously published volume 2 (2010-2015).

Many developments were only possible because those involved in the implementation were also prepared to tread new paths, take risks and often operate with us far outside the norms. I am infinitely grateful that we have found a number of such brave and committed comrades-in-arms, and we still work with many of them today.

Genauso wichtig wie die Zusammenarbeit mit den Ausführenden war und ist von Anfang an der enge und fortwährende Dialog mit unserer Bauherrschaft. Ich brauche das Gespräch mit den Auftraggebern und ich schätze Bauherren, die nicht nur am Resultat, sondern auch am Prozess der Formfindung und der Lösung der Aufgabe interessiert sind. Das ideale Arbeiten findet also in einer Gruppe von Gleichgesinnten statt, die eine Vision teilen und weder Mühe noch Arbeit scheuen. Es ist nicht immer alles leichtgefallen, aber wenn es gelang, einen zielstrebigen Plan, einen Willen sowie geistige und körperliche Arbeit zusammenzubringen, dann war dies für mich immer köstlich.

Produktive und tätige Menschen sind sicher für andere nicht immer bequem, aber da schon eine Nuance den Unterschied zwischen Kunst und Belanglosigkeit bestimmen kann, mussten wir uns immer auf die Re-

Perhaps the fact that we have designed the homes of several of these craftsmen, most recently the **Haus im Weinberg** for one of the two owners of a shell construction company we closely work with, shows that they appreciate this architecture, this way of interacting and working together.

From the very beginning, the close and ongoing dialogue with our clients was just as important as the cooperation with the construction companies. I need to talk to clients and I appreciate clients who are not only interested in the result but also in the process of finding the form and the solution to the brief. So the ideal work takes place in a group of like-minded people who share a vision and spare neither effort nor work. Things have not always come easily, but whenever it was possible to bring together a purposeful plan, a resolve, and mental and physical labour, it was always delightful for me.

geln verlassen und verständigen. Bis heute fällt es mir schwer, Abstriche hinzunehmen, und so bewegen sich die Leitlinien meines Schaffens immer wieder in den gleichen Dimensionen. Deshalb ist dann auch heute ein Haus für mich immer noch nicht nur ein Haus, sondern ein Gemeinschaftswerk, ein geistiger und architektonischer Ort, wo sich Kraft, Natur und Wissenschaft, Kunst und Leben zu einem modellhaften Anspruch verbinden. Gelungen ist dies, wenn die Zuwendung und die Liebe, die hineingegeben wurden, ablesbar und spürbar werden. Dieses Ziel zu erreichen, meine ich, ist nur in einem Prozess möglich, bei dem es viel gegenseitiges Verständnis gibt und der Umgang zwischen allen Beteiligten respektvoll und eher freundschaftlich familiär ist, also genau diese Gruppe von Menschen, die dasselbe Ziel haben. Das Prozesshafte bestimmt bis heute unsere Arbeit, und so hören Planung und Entwicklung erst mit der Fertigstellung auf.

Dieser dritte Band mit sechs aktuellen Wohnhäusern zeigt, dass wir den Weg zu einer gelasseneren und noch mehr dem Leben zugewandten Architektur weiter gegangen sind.

Jahr für Jahr verspüre ich eine zunehmende Freiheit, Elemente und Motive, die wir aus der Geschichte des Bauens kennen, auch in unsere Arbeit aufzunehmen. Die Befreiung von den Dogmen der Moderne lässt uns heute immer mehr von einem starren Bauhaus-Verständnis abrücken und unbeschwerter selbst dekorative und figurative Elemente planen. Gerade bei meinem eigenen Haus versuchte ich, mich von allzu großen Anforderungen an Präzision und Perfektion zu lösen und dem Unbestimmten, aber Sinnlicheren mehr Raum zu geben. Ein Beispiel ist der Kamin, bei dem Platten in die Schalung eingelegt wurden, die beim Ausschalen durch die Haftung zu einem Ausbrechen der verbleibenden Fugen führen würde.

Productive and active people are certainly not always convenient for others, but since even a nuance can determine the difference between art and triviality, we have always had to rely and agree on the rules. To this day, I find it difficult to lower my sights, and so the guidelines of my creative work always remain within the same dimensions. Consequently, even today, a house for me is still not just a house but the result of a joint effort, a spiritual and architectural place where power, nature and science, art and life combine to create an exemplary aspiration. This is successful when the devotion and love that has been incorporated into the house becomes perceptible and tangible.

Achieving this goal, I think, is only possible in a process that is based on great mutual understanding and respectful and almost friendly, familiar interaction between all participants, meaning exactly this group of people sharing the same goal. The processual nature still determines our work today, and that is why planning and developing only ends with completion.

This third volume featuring six recently completed private residences shows that we have continued on the path towards a more serene architecture that is even more in tune with life.

Year after year, I feel an ever-increasing freedom to incorporate almost all the elements we know from the history of building. The further liberation from the dogmas of modern architecture allows us today to move away even further from the Bauhaus idea and to light-heartedly plan decorative and figurative elements. In my own house in particular, I tried to distance myself from too many demands for precision and perfection and to give more room to the indeterminate but more sensual. One example is the fireplace, where panels were inserted into the formwork that would cause the remaining joints to crack due to adhesion when stripping the formwork.

Auch stelle ich fest, dass die Möglichkeiten, etwas Schönes zu erschaffen und es auch als Solches zu bezeichnen, immer mehr werden und dass wir nicht mehr ständig das Gefühl haben, etwas Neues oder nie Dagewesenes entwickeln zu müssen. So gibt es eben diese große Freiheit, die in meinem Gefühl zu einer Art Vollendung führt, weil unser Baukasten eben viel, viel umfassender ist, als er jemals war.

Noch vor der Planung meines Hauses bekamen wir den Auftrag, für die Firma Listone Giordano aus Perugia neue Holzböden in der Reihe Natural Genius zu entwickeln. Bei mir entstand das Bedürfnis, diesem neuen Boden Glanzpunkte hinzuzufügen und ihm dadurch eine Zuwendung zuteil werden zu lassen, die sich aus dem Nutzen nicht zwangsweise ergibt.

Allerdings ist dieses Unternehmen, das eigene Wälder im französischen Fontaine unterhält und diese nachhaltig bewirtschaftet, für seine Eichendielen bekannt. Aus diesen Eichen werden auch Barrique-Fässer gefertigt und diese altern bekanntlich mit einer silberfarben oxidierten Oberfläche. Schon seit Jahrzehnten werden nahezu überall Dielen oder Böden in Dielenoptik verbaut, weil die meisten Menschen damit Wärme und Gemütlichkeit verbinden. Und selbst unsere Bauherren konnte ich nicht immer davon überzeugen, dass ein Dielenboden nicht zwanghaft zu einem bürgerlichen Haus gehört, sondern eher in ein einfaches Bauernhaus.

Mein Wunsch war, einerseits dieses Bedürfnis nach Wärme und Natürlichkeit zu erfüllen und andererseits an mit hoher Handwerkskunst gefertigte Parkettböden mit Intarsien wieder anzuknüpfen. Daraus entstand der Boden **BETWEEN**, der die etwas robustere Anmutung einer Diele mit der Feinheit eines klassischen Intarsienparketts in einem zwanglosen Zusammenspiel zu einer zeitgemäßen Synthese verbindet. Er ist gemacht für moderne, offene und fließende Raumkonzepte und lässt

I also notice that the possibilities to create something beautiful and to also describe it as such are increasing and that we no longer constantly feel the need to develop something new or unprecedented. Hence, there is this great freedom, which I feel leads to a kind of completion, because our toolbox is much more comprehensive than it has ever been.

Before I started planning my house, we were commissioned by Listone Giordano from Perugia to develop new wood floors for their Natural Genius range. I felt the need to add highlights to this new flooring and thus to give it attention that is not dictated by its usefulness.

On the other hand, the company, which maintains and sustainably manages its own forests in Fontaine, France, is known for its oak floorboards. These oaks are also used to manufacture barrique barrels, which acquire a silvery oxidised surface with age. For decades, floor-

boards or flooring with wood look have been installed almost everywhere because most people associate them with warmth and cosiness. I have not always been able to convince even our clients that plank flooring does not necessarily belong in a bourgeois house but rather in a simple farmhouse.

On the one hand, I wanted to fulfil this need for warmth and naturalness and, on the other hand, I wanted to take up the tradition of parquet floors with marquetry, which are manufactured with a high level of craftsmanship. This resulted in the **BETWEEN** flooring, which combines

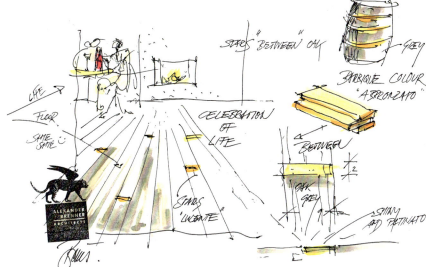

sich durch die unterschiedlichen Stabbreiten von 140 und 90 Millimetern auch leicht an verschiedene Raummaße anpassen. Das Eichenholz wird mit einer Reaktivbeize behandelt, die mit der Gerbsäure der Eiche reagiert und den warmen grauen Farbton entstehen lässt. Zwischen die schmaleren Stäbe werden in losen Abständen massive Messingelemente eingelegt, die gänzlich unbehandelt sind und im Lauf der Zeit materialtypisch oxidieren.

Ich beschreibe diesen Boden hier etwas ausführlicher, weil er zeigt, wie wir heute an die Dinge herangehen. Ohne den schon erwähnten Zwang, etwas noch nie Dagewesenes zu schaffen, kann etwas entstehen, das vertraut wirkt und trotzdem in seiner Art und Verbindung ganz neu ist. Holz und Messing, eine Liaison gegensätzlicher Materialien in einer spielerischen, heiteren Leichtigkeit vereint.

Ein weiteres Beispiel für diese Herangehensweise ist auch das Daybed **KAP** aus dem Jahr 2019, welches ein Polster in klassischer Kapitonierung erhielt. Um es flexibel nutzen zu können, wurden Rollen hinter dem konischen Messingsockel angebracht. In eine Fuge zwischen Sockel und Polster können an jeder Stelle Seitentische und Ablagen für Gläser, aber auch für Notebooks oder Tablets eingeschoben werden. Dies macht dieses Möbel zu einem zeitgemäßen, flexiblen Lieblingsstück, das sogar leicht in den Außenbereich gerollt werden kann. Diese Neuinterpretation steht bei ähnlicher Anmutung somit den klassischen, oft schweren und unverrückbaren Chesterfield-Möbeln gegenüber.

the somewhat more robust look of a floorboard with the subtlety of a classic marquetry parquet in an informal interplay to create a contemporary synthesis. It is designed for modern, open and flowing spatial concepts and can be easily adapted to the room dimensions thanks to the different slat widths of 140 and 90 mm. The oak wood is treated with a greying stain, which reacts with the tannic acid of the oak and creates the warm grey colour. Solid brass elements are inserted at loose intervals between the narrower slats. These are completely untreated and oxidise over time as is typical for this material.

The reason I describe this particular flooring in more detail is that it shows how we approach things today, namely without the previously mentioned pressure of having to create something that has never been seen before. But it is precisely from this that things can emerge that seem familiar and yet are completely new in their nature and combination. Wood and brass, a liaison of contrasting materials united in a playful, cheerful lightness.

Another example of this approach is the **KAP** daybed from 2019, which was given an upholstery with classic deep button tufting. To allow flexible use, castors were attached behind the conical brass base and side tables and shelves for glasses, but also for notebooks or tablets, can be inserted into a joint between the base and the upholstery at any point. This makes this furniture a contemporary, flexible favourite that can even be easily moved outdoors. This new interpretation thus contrasts with the classic, often heavy and immovable Chesterfield sofas, while retaining a similar appearance.

Of course, we have also worked on a large number of projects that are not extensively documented in the main part of this volume, but which have also enabled us to take steps forward; precisely those projects that are slightly outside the scope of our day-to-day activities.

Natürlich haben wir auch an einer großen Zahl von Projekten gearbeitet, die hier im Hauptteil dieses Bandes nicht umfänglich dokumentiert sind, die uns aber auch vorangebracht haben. Das sind eben häufig Projekte, die ein wenig außerhalb unseres alltäglichen Tuns liegen. Gerade bei solchen Projekten, wie beispielsweise Umbauten oder innenarchitektonischen Aufgaben, sind wir immer wieder gezwungen, uns mit einem Bestand auseinanderzusetzen. Wir haben große Freude daran, diese Herausforderungen anzunehmen und dabei zu lernen. In den 25 Jahren, in denen wir hauptsächlich privaten Wohnungsbau machen, haben wir versucht, pro Jahr mindestens auch ein Projekt zu machen, das mit unserer klassischen Arbeit wenig oder gar nichts zu tun hat. Diese Projekte publizieren wir meist nicht, um zu vermeiden, weitere Anfragen für ähnliche Aufgaben oder Folgeaufträge dieser Art zu erhalten. Dies würde unsere Kapazitäten übersteigen. Die tatsächlich von uns bearbeiteten Umbauten kommen deshalb von unseren Bestandsbauherrschaften oder aus dem engeren Freundeskreis, oder eben von jemandem, mit dem wir schon seit vielen Jahren zusammenarbeiten. So verhielt es sich auch bei dem Haus **Submarine**, dessen Name einerseits eine Anspielung auf die Eigentümer ist, aber andererseits auch auf ein Projekt unter dem Radar, also abgetaucht.

Umso mehr Freude machte es, für die Familie eines unserer Handwerker mit fünf Kindern, in einem wohlwollenden, freundschaftlichen Klima eine Renovierung und einen Anbau zu planen. Bei diesem Projekt, bei dem ja unterschwellig das Thema U-Boot mitschwang, entstand im Anbau, einem großen Familienraum mit Küche, Essen und Wohnen ein raumgliederndes Objekt, das in seiner Form an ein U-Boot oder dessen Kommandoturm erinnert. Ich glaube, dass dies einer der ersten Raumeinbauten war, bei dem Rundungen überwiegen. Ich beschreibe das deshalb gern, weil auch dies zeigt,

Especially with such projects, for example conversions or interior design assignments, we are always forced to deal with things and an existing building, and we take great pleasure in accepting these challenges and learning in the process. For the past 25 years, during which we have mainly done private housing construction, we have tried to do at least one project per year that has little or nothing to do with our classic line of work.

If possible, we do not publish these projects in order to avoid possible requests for similar tasks or follow-up commissions, as this would exceed our capacities. The conversions we actually work on are either commissioned by our existing clients or from our close circle of friends, or from someone with whom we have been working for many years. This was also the case with the **Submarine** house, whose name is on the one hand an allusion to the owners, but on the other hand to a project below the radar, in other words, submerged.

This makes it all the more enjoyable for us to renovate and build an extension for one of our craftsmen and his family with five children in a friendly and benevolent atmosphere. In this project, in which the submarine theme resonated subliminally, a space-structuring object was

wie in einem evolutionären Prozess Dinge zunächst gedacht werden, dann ausprobiert, ihre Raumwirkung und ihre Funktionalität begutachtet und sie dann Bestandteil unseres Repertoires werden. Rundungen, vor allem im Arbeits- und Bewegungsbereich, zum Beispiel auch in Küchen, sind in unseren Arbeiten immer häufiger anzutreffen, so beim Küchenblock im Rudolph House, beim Portus House und beim Rutschenhaus, einem in Fertigstellung befindlichen Umbau eines Hauses aus den Zwanzigerjahren.

Wir nennen es **Rutschenhaus**, weil es in der neu geschaffenen zentralen Halle parallel zur geschwungenen Treppe eine Rutsche gibt.

Wir freuen uns, wenn unsere Bauherrschaft außergewöhnliche Ideen hat, und haben großen Spaß daran, diese dann auch umzusetzen. Dies öffnet den Blick und erweitert die Möglichkeiten, immer wieder neue maßgeschneiderte Gesamtwerke zu schaffen. Tatsächlich haben wir schon viele Treppen ausgeführt, jedoch bisher ohne begleitende Rutsche. Wir waren überrascht, wie viele Menschen, nachdem sie das gesehen hatten, nicht mehr verstanden, warum sie selbst keine Rutsche haben, ja warum es überhaupt erlaubt ist, Treppen ohne Rutsche zu bauen. Jemand war sogar der Meinung, dass Rutschen baurechtlich verpflichtend werden müssten.

Junge und ältere Menschen sind davon angetan und sogar Personen mit Knieleiden sehen darin große Vorteile. Wir lieben es, Menschen so zu berühren und das Kind in ihnen zu wecken.

Es ist schön, mit der 100 Jahre alten Bausubstanz umzugehen und zu sehen, wie nachhaltig und solide in technischer, aber auch in gestalterischer Hinsicht damals gearbeitet wurde. Wir hoffen und wünschen uns auch für unsere heutigen Bauten, dass sie denen, die sie einst um- oder weiterbauen, eine genauso gute Grundlage sind.

created in the extension, a large family room with kitchen, dining and living areas, whose shape is reminiscent of a submarine or its conning tower. I think this was one of the first room fixtures that is predominately characterised by its curved silhouette. I like to describe this because it also shows how, in an evolutionary process, things are first conceived, then tried out; how their spatial effect and functionality are examined and they then become part of our repertoire. Rounded shapes, especially in the areas where people work and move, such as in a kitchen, are increasingly to be found in our work, for example the kitchen blocks in the Rudolph House, the Portus House and the Rutschenhaus, a conversion of a house from the 1920s that is currently being completed.

We call this house **Rutschenhaus** (slide house) because there is a slide in the newly created central hall that runs parallel to the sweeping staircase.

We are delighted when our clients have unusual ideas and very much enjoy implementing them. This broadens our horizons and expands our possibilities for creating new bespoke total works of art again and again. Well, we have already built many staircases, but none with an accompanying slide. We were surprised how many people who saw this design solution no longer understood why they themselves did not have a slide installed and that it is even permitted to build stairs without a slide. One person was even of the opinion that this should be obligatory under building law.

Both the young and the old are taken with it and even people with knee problems see great benefits. We love moving people emotionally and awakening the child in them.

Schon länger beschäftigt uns das **Lake House**, das nun zur Ausführung kam, direkt am Bodensee gelegen. Das Grundstück wird seeseitig von fünf riesigen Pappeln dominiert, die sich mit dem Seeblick überlagern und einen ganz besonderen Zauber erzeugen. Auch dieses Haus ist ein Umbau, allerdings stammt der Bestand aus den Sechzigerjahren des letzten Jahrhunderts. Auch hier wieder eine spannende Herausforderung, zumal wir uns dadurch mit dem Thema einer Fassadenbekleidung befassen mussten. Diese wurde dann in sägerauer, gekalkter und anschließend rosé lasierter Eiche ausgeführt. Da es sich um das Ferienhaus einer unserer langjährigen Bauherrschaften handelt, hatten wir die Möglichkeit, offen und experimentell zu arbeiten und sowohl zeittypische Bestandsmerkmale, wie den Kamin zu erhalten und auf der anderen Seite Spuren der Veränderung zu thematisieren. Das neue, runde Oberlicht im Wohnbereich wurde aus organisatorischen Gründen herausgestemmt und nicht, wie sonst, gesägt. Wir haben die Bruchstelle der Bohrungen vergoldet und ein rosé-farbenes Oberlicht aufgesetzt. So etwas ist nur möglich, weil wir auch auf der Baustelle architektonische Verantwortung übernehmen und dadurch solch ein Stück Lebensfreude entstehen kann. Das Besondere und das Schöne sind kaum fassbar und oft im Augenblick ein Mythos, aber für uns eine der wichtigsten Gewissheiten in der Architektur überhaupt.

It is wonderful to treat the 100-year-old building fabric and to see how sustainable and solid the work was back then in terms of technology, but also in terms of design. We hope and wish for our current buildings that they will be just as good a foundation for those who once converted or extend them.

Another project that we have been working on for some time, but which has now been completed, is the **Lake House**, located directly on Lake Constance. Five huge poplars dominate the lake side of the property, overlapping with the lake view and creating a very special magic. This house, too, is a conversion, though the original building dates back to the 1960s. Again, this was an exciting challenge, especially as it meant we had to deal with the issue of a façade cladding. This was executed in sawn, whitewashed oak finished with a rosé glaze. As this is the holiday home of one of our long-standing clients, we had the opportunity to work openly and experimentally and, on the one hand, to retain features typical of the period, such as the fireplace, and, on the other hand, to make traces of change a design theme. For organisational reasons, the new, circular skylight in the living area was chiselled out and not, as usual, sawn. We gilded the broken part of the drill holes and installed a rosé-coloured skylight. Such details are only possible because we also take architectural responsibility on the building site, and this is how such a piece of joie de vivre can emerge. The special and the beautiful are hardly tangible and often a myth at the very moment, but for us, they are one of the most important certainties in architecture altogether.

Im letzten Buch hatte ich über den Anlass für die Planung der **Parler Residences PR41** geschrieben. Ebenso darüber, dass nicht alle Menschen in einem Einfamilienhaus leben möchten und wir deshalb einen Geschosswohnungsbau planten, der etwas abweichend von allzu prozessoptimierten Bauträgerprojekten, eher wieder Werte in den Vordergrund stellt, wie sie bei Gründerzeithäusern noch üblich waren.

So sind der Zugang und auch die Gemeinschaftsflächen großzügig bemessen und sie haben Aufenthaltsqualitäten. Es ist ein Ort geworden, an dem man gerne wohnt. Da sich auf jeder Etage nur eine Wohnung befindet, verspüren die Bewohner ein ausgewogenes Maß zwischen Öffentlichkeit und hoher Privatheit. Seitliche Einblicke sind dadurch vermieden, dass auf der Südwestseite das komplett geschlossene Brenner Research House anschließt und auf der gegenüberliegenden Seite der alte Baumbestand erhalten wurde. Durch die geschlossenen Brüstungen sind die Bewohner vor Einblicken aus dem Straßenraum geschützt, auch das Erdgeschoss liegt oberhalb der vorgelagerten Garagen, also eigentlich schon im Obergeschoss. Die langen, ruhigen Brüstungen zur Straße hin erzeugen eine klare Raumwand und ragen über die an den Stirnseiten liegenden loggienartigen Freisitze hinaus. Die zurückgesetzten Schlafzimmer öffnen sich zu diesen Terrassen, sodass sich alle Räume außer den Bädern zur Tal- und Aussichtsseite hin orientieren. Küche, Essen und Wohnen sind in einem loftartigen, großen Raum über die ganze Hausbreite angeordnet. Dies schafft ein großzügiges, elegantes Wohngefühl.

In the last book, I wrote about the reason for planning the **Parler Residences PR41**. I also wrote about the fact that not everyone wants to live in a single-family house and that we therefore planned a multi-storey apartment building that, in a slight departure from overly process-optimised property development projects, puts the emphasis back on values that were still common in Wilhelminian-style houses.

The entrance and the communal areas are generously proportioned and have high amenity qualities. It has become a place where people enjoy living, and because there is only one flat on each floor, the residents feel a balance between the public sphere and a high degree of privacy. Views into the building from the side are avoided by the completely enclosed Brenner Research House adjoining on the south-west side and the old trees on the opposite side. The closed parapets also protect the residents from views from the street, and even the ground floor is actually situated on the first floor, i.e. above the garages in front. The long, calm parapets facing the street create a distinct definition and project out over the loggia-like outdoor seating areas on the sides. The set-back bedrooms open onto these terraces, so that all rooms except the bathrooms are oriented towards the valley side affording panoramic views. The kitchen, dining and living areas are arranged in a loft-like large room spanning the entire width of the house. This creates a generous, elegant sense of living.

I would like to present two more projects that we have recently completed under the leitmotif of conciseness and a cultivated way of life. The villa in the countryside, for over 2,000 years synonymous with living on a spacious plot of land, has always been an experimental laboratory under ideal conditions, but also a great challenge in dealing with the landscape.

Zwei jüngst fertiggestellte Projekte möchte ich noch unter dem Thema Prägnanz und kultivierte Lebensart vorstellen. Die Villa auf dem Land, seit über 2000 Jahren Synonym für das Leben auf weitem Grundstück, war schon immer ein Versuchslabor unter idealen Voraussetzungen, aber auch eine große Herausforderung im Umgang mit der Landschaft.

Das **Portus House** in Pforzheim durften wir in einem solchen Landschaftsgarten planen, der aufgrund seines Bestands die Lage und Orientierung des Hauses praktisch vorgab. Positioniert am Nordrand des Grundstücks öffnen sich das Haus und seine Terrassen auf drei Seiten zur Natur. Entfernt liegende Nachbargebäude wurden durch Geländemodulation und gezielte Neupflanzung von Großgehölzen ausgeblendet. Das Haus für einen Menschen, der sein Leben mit dem Erfinden von Schönem verbringt, hier mit dem Erschaffen von Schmuck, sollte Zeugnis von den Lebensgewohnheiten seiner Erbauer, aber vor allem Zeugnis von der Kultur seiner Zeit ablegen. Ein Thema, das uns durch unsere ganze Arbeit begleitet: Was ist der bürgerliche Bau heute und was kann er, wenn überhaupt, gesellschaftlich beitragen? Wir leiten daraus die Pflicht ab, zeitgemäße Schönheit zu erschaffen und abseits des regelbasierten, alltäglichen Baugeschehens neue und alte Bauweisen, aber auch Materialien auszuprobieren. Wir sehen dies als eine Art Zusammenschau,

We had the privilege of planning the **Portus House** in Pforzheim in such a landscape garden, the existing features of which practically predetermined the location and orientation of the house. Positioned on the northern edge of the site, the house and its terraces open up towards nature on three sides. Distant neighbouring buildings were hidden by modulating the terrain accordingly and by deliberately planting new large trees and shrubs. The house for a person who spends his life inventing beautiful objects, that is, the creation of jewellery, had to bear witness to the lifestyle habits of its owners, but above all, to the culture of its time.

A theme that accompanies us throughout our work: what is the bourgeois building today and what, if anything, can it contribute to society? From this, we derive the obligation to create contemporary beauty and to try out new and old building methods, but also materials, outside of the rule-based, everyday building process. We see this as a kind of synopsis in which we can access all the technical possibilities of contemporary architec-

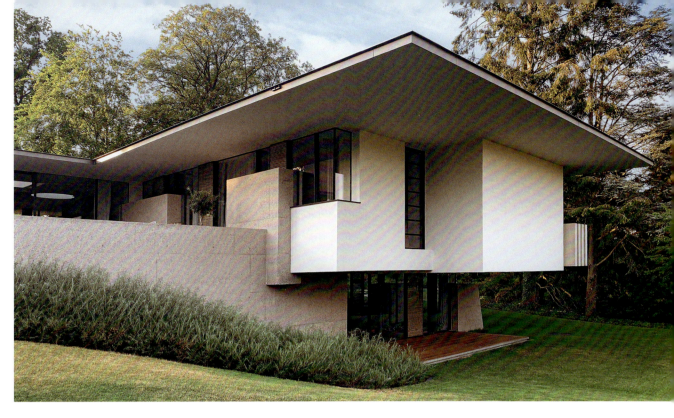

bei der wir auf alle technischen Möglichkeiten der Gegenwartsarchitektur zugreifen können, aber ebenso grundsätzliche menschliche Bedürfnisse berücksichtigen und gleichzeitig ein Werk der Schönheit, welches die Natur so nicht verwirklichen kann, schaffen.

Die besondere Verantwortung, auf einem solchen Grundstück arbeiten zu können, stand auch bei unserem Projekt **Parkside House** an erster Stelle. Es sollte dort ein möglichst einfacher, eingeschossiger Bungalow für eine Familie entstehen. Ein Bautypus wie etwa der Kanzlerbungalow von Sep Ruf war der Wunsch, und so realisierten wir das Leben und Wohnen auf einer Etage. Lediglich Technik und Nebenräume sowie ein Gästebereich sind in dem aus dem Hang hervortretenden Sockelgeschoss untergebracht. Die Räume des täglichen Lebens wie Hauswirtschaft, Wohnküche und Eingangshalle orientieren sich zu einem gepflasterten Platz auf der Nordseite. Essen, Wohnen und Bibliothek, sowie der Spielbereich der Kinder lagern um die große Terrasse nach Südwesten, die in den Sommermonaten, beschützt vom weit auskragenden Dach, zum Hauptlebensraum wird. Alle privaten und die Schlafräume hingegen orientieren sich zur ruhigen Ostseite. Im Alltag bestens dienlich ist ein zurückhaltender, ruhiger und schöner Ort des Lebens entstanden – ein Stück Heimat.

ture, yet also take into account fundamental human needs, while simultaneously achieving a work of beauty that nature cannot create in this way. The special responsibility associated with having the opportunity to work on such a plot of land was also paramount in our **Parkside House** project.

The idea was to build a straightforward, single-storey bungalow for a family. The client wanted a building type resembling the Chancellor's bungalow by Sep Ruf, and so we realised living and dwelling on one floor. Only building services and ancillary rooms, as well as a guest area, are located in the base level, which protrudes from the slope. The rooms for day-to-day living, such as housekeeping area, kitchen and entrance hall, are oriented towards a paved square on the north side. The dining, living and library areas, along with the children's play area, are arranged around the large terrace facing southwest, which is the main living space in the summer months, protected by the wide cantilevered roof. All private rooms and bedrooms, on the other hand, are oriented towards the quiet east side. A modest, quiet and beautiful place to live has been created that serves everyday life perfectly – a piece of home.

HERE ON FELLBACH 2027

Die Projekte auf den vorangegangenen Seiten sind zwar fertiggestellt, aber noch nicht ausführlich dokumentiert und fotografiert. Andere Projekte, die uns derzeit intensiv beschäftigen, sind noch in einer ganz frühen Konzeptphase, und so gibt es davon nur erste Zeichnungen.

Und wie schon beschrieben, machen wir auch immer Projekte, die uns besonders herausfordern. Eines davon ist **HERE ON**, die Konversion eines Areals mit einer Grundfläche von 34.000 Quadratmetern an einer spannenden Nahtstelle zwischen einem Streifen verbliebener Agrarlandschaft und aufgelassenem Industriegebiet. Direkt an der Gemarkungsgrenze zwischen Stuttgart und Fellbach gelegen, gibt es hier die Möglichkeit, ein modernes Stadttor zu schaffen, das den Bogen zum Hochhaus am gegenüberliegenden östlichen Stadtende spannt. Wir freuen uns, dass unser Konzept mit dem Erhalt und der Umnutzung eines zeittypischen Industrieunternehmens aus den Sechzigerjahren, verbunden mit einem Klinikneubau und einem Hochhaus an der Stuttgarter Straße breite Zustimmung fand. Auch wenn die verbleibende Zeit knapp sein wird, soll das Projekt Teil der Internationalen Bauausstellung IBA'27 in Stuttgart werden.

Auch an vielen weiteren spannenden Projekten arbeiten wir derzeit, darunter weitere Einfamilienwohnhäuser. Dieser Bautypus ermöglicht es uns, unsere Sehnsucht nach dem Gesamtwerk am besten zu stillen, denn bei keiner anderen Bauaufgabe gibt es die Möglichkeit, nahezu ohne weitere Beteiligte dieses Werk als Ganzheit zu planen, eben mit allen Belangen des Bauwerks. So inte-

The projects on the previous pages have been completed, but not yet extensively documented and photographed. Other projects that are currently occupying us intensively are still in a very early concept phase and hence all that we have are first sketches and drawings.

As I already mentioned, we also always work on projects that are particularly challenging. One of these is **HERE ON**, the conversion of a 34,000-square-metre site at an exciting interface between a strip of remaining agricultural landscape and a former industrial area. Situated directly on the boundary between Stuttgart and the town of Fellbach, the opportunity arises to create a modern gateway to the city that forges a visual bridge to the high-rise building on the opposite eastern side of the city. We are pleased that the concept with the partial preservation and conversion of a 1960s industrial company building typical of its time, combined with the construction of a new hospital building and a high-rise on Stuttgarter Strasse, met with broad approval. Even though the remaining time is going to be tight, the project is to become part of the International Building Exhibition IBA'27 in Stuttgart.

In addition, we are currently working on many other exciting projects, including more single-family homes. This type of building allows us to best satisfy our longing for the total work of art, because no other building task gives us the opportunity to plan a building in its entirety, including all aspects of the building, with almost no other parties involved. I am interested in our houses as elements of the city, but also

ressieren mich unsere Häuser als Bausteine der Stadt, aber auch als freistehende Skulptur. Der hervorgebrachten Schönheit eine Dauer zu geben ist die logische Konsequenz, und deshalb haben wir ein ganz natürliches Verhältnis zur und Bedürfnis nach Nachhaltigkeit im reinen Wortsinn. Ich glaube weiterhin, dass es richtig ist, alle Dinge mit großer Hingabe zu planen und auch auszuführen. Die Firma Porsche wirbt damit, dass 70 Prozent aller jemals von ihnen gebauten Autos heute noch fahren. Und ich glaube, der Grund ist auch dort, dass niemand Interesse daran verspürt, sich von etwas zu trennen, das technische Perfektion und Schönheit vereint. Auch eine große Zahl von Villen aller Epochen steht heute noch, weil sich immer jemand findet, der ihren Wert erkennt und schätzt, und sie noch pflegt und unterhält, selbst wenn die Nutzung sich längst geändert hat.

Das Haus als Gesamtwerk muss aber nicht nur schön und handwerklich gut gemacht sein, sondern es muss zuvorderst dem Bewohner dienen und im Alltag höchst gebrauchsfähig sein. Im Vorausdenken und im täglichen gedanklichen Durchleben der Projekte versuchen wir, dies als Ganzes zu durchdringen, so dass die Ordnung der Zusammenhänge in der Übertragung auf andere gelingt. Aber was ist das Ganze? Für uns ist es die Obsession, die Räume, die Flächen, die Einbauten, die Möbel, das Licht, aber auch die Technik auf diesen spezifischen Ort maßzuschneidern und alles zusammen mit dem Außenraum zu einer Einheit so zu formen, dass alle Sinne im Einklang angesprochen werden. Die Kraft der gedanklichen Konzentration auf das Ganze, der Mut und das Wollen sind die Voraussetzung, aber Wirklichkeit wird das Gesamtkunstwerk eben nur durch die entschlossenen Mitstreiter, die es dann mit Leidenschaft und all ihrem Wissen und Können in die Welt bringen.

as free-standing sculptures. Giving the beauty that has been created a lasting quality is the logical consequence, which is why we have a very natural relationship to and need for sustainability in the pure sense of the word. Furthermore, I believe that it is the right approach to plan things once with great dedication and also to execute them that way. The Porsche company advertises the fact that 70% of all the cars they have ever built are still running today, and I believe that this is also the reason why, when technical perfection is combined with beauty, no one is interested in parting with them. A large number of villas from all eras still exist today because there is always someone who recognises and appreciates their value and also cares for and maintains them, even if their original use has long since changed.

However, the house as a total work of art must not only be beautiful and well-crafted, but it must first and foremost serve the occupant and be highly functional in everyday life. In thinking ahead and going through the projects in our minds every day, we try to penetrate them as a whole, so that the order of the interrelationships succeeds when transferred to others. But what is the whole? For us it is the obsession to customise the rooms, the surfaces, the fixtures, the furniture, the lighting, but also the technical equipment for this specific place and to bring everything together with the outside space to form a unity in a way that appeals to all the senses in unison. The power of focusing one's thoughts on the whole, the courage and the will are the prerequisites, but the total work of art only becomes a reality with the determined comrades-in-arms who then bring it into the world with passion and all their knowledge and skills.

LIST OF WORKS
1990 – 2008

Centrale
bar
Stuttgart 1990 – 1991

Schneider
penthouse
Stuttgart 1990 – 1991

Binder
atelier for metal design
Suessen 1990 – 1991

Scharnhauser Park
master plan, residential development
Ostfildern 1991

Dr. Wörwag
private residence, conversion
Stuttgart 1991

Orfeu Negro
club
Bielefeld 1991 – 1992

Wernhalde
private residence
Stuttgart 1990 – 1992

TV-Kohlensäure
company building
Ludwigshafen 1992

Calwer Jewels
jeweller
Stuttgart 1993

Dessous
dessous shop
Stuttgart 1993

A Loft
loft
Asperg 1993

Döringer
private residence
Stuttgart 1992 – 1994

TV-Kohlensäure
company building
Plochingen 1993 – 1994

Sonderbar
bar & restaurant
Stuttgart 1994

Zucca
restaurant
Stuttgart 1994

PDX Music
recording studio
Stuttgart 1994

Kookai
fashion store
Stuttgart 1994

B Loft
loft, design
Ludwigsburg 1994

B Lake House
private residence, project
Lake Starnberg 1994 – 1995

Schütte
restaurant
Rottenburg 1994 – 1995

Salomon
flat
Salach 1994 – 1995

K House
private residence, design
Hechingen 1995

Bulachweg
housing estate, design
Warmbronn 1995

Küenle
private residence, conversion
Stuttgart 1995

Duerr
private residence, conversion
Stuttgart 1995 – 1996

Sten House
private residence, project
Munich 1995 – 1996

Trepte
commercial | residential building, project
Dresden 1996

Project Development Company
office
Rottenburg 1996

Dr. A House
private residence, design
Stuttgart 1996

TV-Kohlensäure
company building, project
Frankfurt am Main 1996

Inova
office
Stuttgart 1997

W House
private residence, design
Ulm 1997

Zacher
flat
Stuttgart 1997

R6 House
private residence
Stuttgart 1996 – 1998

CAS House
commercial building, conversion
Reutlingen 1998

Dr. Eisele
office
Rottenburg 1998

Sauter - Stodal
penthouse
Echterdingen 1998

Robo
private residence
Stuttgart 1997 – 1999

Kaiser
private residence, design
Hailfingen 1999

WBW
two apartment houses, design
Stuttgart 2000

Miki 3
duplex town house
Stuttgart 1998 – 2000

Am Oberen Berg
private residence, design
Stuttgart 1999 – 2000

Dino
company headquarters, project
Stuttgart 2000

Miki 1
duplex residence
Stuttgart 2000 – 2002

K7 House
private residence
Stuttgart 2000 – 2002

Weyrich
loft
Stuttgart 2002

Bop
private residence
Gerlingen 2001 – 2003

Auf der Alb
country residence
Heroldstatt 2002 – 2003

Miki 21
private residence
Stuttgart 2002 – 2003

Dr. Wörwag
library addition
Stuttgart 2003

Erl
private residence, design
Regensburg 2003

Villa V
private residence, design
Marbella 2003

Dornhalde
small residential tower
Stuttgart 2002 – 2004

Hawk
private residence
Munich 2004 – 2005

LH 2
flat
Stuttgart 2005

B-Wald
woodland residence
Stuttgart 2004 – 2006

Ausgezeichnete Architektur in Baden-Württemberg
exhibition, Stuttgart 2006

Am Oberen Berg
private residence
Stuttgart 2004 – 2007

Am Schlossberg
two private residences, project
Gerlingen 2007

W 29
private residence
Esslingen 2005 – 2007

New Architecture in Stuttgart
travelling exhibition
worldwide 2006 – 2007

Parrotta Contemporary Art
art gallery
Stuttgart 2007

B 82
private residence
Stuttgart 2006 – 2008

Conte
bar & restaurant
Stuttgart 2008

Heidehof
private residence
Stuttgart 2006 – 2008

Robo
private residence, conversion
Stuttgart 2007 – 2008

LIST OF WORKS
2008 – 2022

Houses
exhibition, Parrotta Contemporary Art
Stuttgart 2008

Houses and Rooms
exhibition, project space Berlin
Berlin 2008

Con House
private residence
Kirchheim 2006 – 2009

Vent House
private residence
Kirchheim 2007 – 2009

Strauss
duplex residence
Stuttgart 2007 – 2009

Mercedes Benz
E-Class set design
Stuttgart 2008

Vista
private residence
Stuttgart 2009 – 2012

King House
private residence, design
Berlin 2009

Houses 1990-2010
exhibition, AIT Salon Munich
Munich 2011

Houses 1990-2010
exhibition, Parrotta Contemporary Art
Stuttgart 2011

Robo
private residence, conversion
Stuttgart 2011 – 2012

SU House
private residence
Stuttgart 2008 – 2012

Lake House
private residence, design
Lake Constance 2011 – 2012

Ausgezeichnete Häuser
exhibition, BDA Wechselraum
Stuttgart 2012

SOL House
private residence
Stuttgart 2010 – 2013

Andro
coffee table, 2013

Submarine
private residence, extension
Stuttgart 2011 – 2013

SEA
mini pool, 2014

Jean P.
table, 2014

An der Achalm
private residence
Reutlingen 2009 – 2014

Irmgard and Karlheinz
bench, 2014

Mercedes-Benz Speedlab
project
Stuttgart 2014

Seehof Hotel
luxury hotel & spa, design
Bad Wiessee 2014

Bredeney House
private residence
Essen 2010 – 2015

One Fine Day
dresser, 2015

Rottmann House
private residence
Wiesbaden 2010 – 2015

Countryside Residence
private residence
Ludwigsburg 2012 – 2015

Im Weinberg
private residence
Ludwigsburg 2013 – 2015

Give and take
tray, 2015

At the creek
landscaping and gardening
Sauerland 2015

Angel - Garder moi dans tes ailes
chair with wings, 2015

Villas and Houses 2010-2015
exhibition, Parrotta Contemporary Art
Stuttgart 2016

   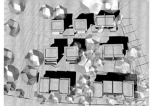 

Haus am Wald
private residence
Stuttgart 2014 – 2016

Am Westerberg
private residence, design
Osnabrück 2014 – 2016

Montafon Haus
private residence, design
Montafon 2016

B-Wald
woodland residence, extension
Stuttgart 2016 – 2017

Crown House
private residence
Frankfurt 2012 – 2017

Between
parquet flooring, 2017 - 2018

JUNG Out of Africa
light switch design, 2018

Schunck
company entrance hall
executive suite
Laufen 2018

Brenner Research House
private residence and atelier
Stuttgart 2015 – 2018

Lightship
lamp, 2018

Conte
parquet flooring, 2018

Flightship
floating shelf, 2019

Fineway House
private residence
Reutlingen 2016 - 2019

Cesare | Cesarino
glass mosaic, 2019

Little Wing
hanger, 2019

S Houses
private residences, concept
Lake Starnberg 2019

KAP
daybed, 2019

Liberty 15
residential tower, concept
Stuttgart 2019

Parler Research House PR41
apartment house
Stuttgart 2015 - 2020

Klinik Dambach
clinic, design
Dambach 2020

Rudolph House
private residence
Stuttgart 2017 - 2021

Parkside House
private residence
Melsungen 2017 – 2022

Housing Estate in the Park
residential estate, concept
Fürth 2021

Black F
private residence
Neuenbürg 2017 - 2022

Portus House
private residence
Pforzheim 2018 - 2022

Lake House
private residence
Lake Constance 2019 - 2022

Rutschenhaus
private residence, conversion
Stuttgart 2020 - 2022

Tank House
private residence
Waiblingen 2020 - 2023

Zastrow House
urban villa
Stuttgart 2021 - 2025

Radikale Mitte
restaurant
Fellbach 2022 - 2023

HERE ON
urban planning project
Fellbach 2022 - 2023

Hasenberg
apartment building
Stuttgart 2022 - 2024

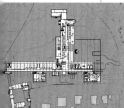    

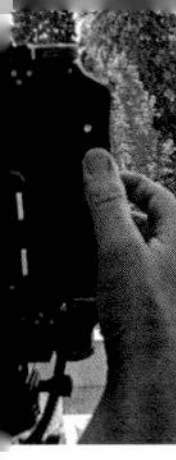        

Photographs Zooey Braun, Stuttgart: Cover, 8, 19, 24/25, 26, 27-2, 28/29, 30/31, 32/33, 34/35, 36/37, 38/39, 40, 41, 42/43, 47, 48, 51, 52/53, 54/55, 56, 58-1, 59-1, 59-3, 60/61, 62, 63, 64, 65, 66/67, 68-1, 68-2, 69-2, 70/71, 73, 76/77, 78/79, 80/81, 82/83, 84, 85, 86, 87, 89, 90/91, 92, 93, 94, 96/97, 98, 99, 100/101, 102-1, 102-4, 102-5, 103, 104, 105, 106/107, 110/111, 119, 120/121, 122/123, 127-2, 129, 130, 132, 133, 134, 135-1, 136, 138, 139, 140/141, 142, 143, 144, 145, 146, 147, 148/149, 150, 151, 152, 153, 154, 155, 157-2, 158/159, 160, 161, 162, 163, 166, 167, 168, 169, 170, 171, 172/173, 174/175, 176/177, 178/179, 180, 181, 182, 183, 184/185, 187, 192/193, 194/195, 196, 197, 198, 200, 201, 202/203, 204, 205, 206, 207, 208, 209, 210, 211, 212, 214, 215, 216-1, 217, 218/219, 220/221, 223, 224/225, 227-7, 229-1, 230, 231, 232/233, 234, 235, 236/237, 239,242/243, 244, 245, 246, 248, 249, 250/251, 252, 253, 254, 255-2, 255-3, 255-8, 256, 257, 258, 259, 260/261, 262/263, 265, 270/271, 274, 275, 276, 278, 279, 280/281, 282, 283, 285-1, 286/287, 289, 290/291, 292/293, 294/295, 297, 298/299, 300/301, 306-4, 307, 311, 317-1, 317-3, 317-4, 317-10, 317-11, 318-1, 318-2, 318-3, 318-4, 318-5, 318-6, 318-7, 318-8, 320-3

Photographs B-and, Alexander Brenner Architects, Stuttgart: 2/3, 27-1, 46, 49, 50, 57-1, 57-2, 58-2, 58-3, 59-2, 69-1, 88, 102-2, 102-3, 102-6, 109, 113, 124, 125, 126, 127-1, 127-3, 127-4, 128, 131, 135-2, 137, 156,157-1, 157-3, 157-4, 164, 165, 199, 213, 216-2, 216-3, 222, 226, 227-1, 227-2, 227-3, 227-4, 227-5, 227-6, 227-8, 227-9, 227-10, 227-11, 228, 229-2, 229-3, 247, 255-1, 25-4, 255-5, 255-6, 255-7, 255-9, 272, 273, 277, 284, 285-2, 285-3, 285-4, 285-5, 285-6, 285-7, 288, 304, 306-1,306-2, 305, 306-3, 308, 309, 310, 312, 313, 314, 315, 316-1, 316-2, 316-3, 316-4, 316-5, 316-7, 316-8, 316-9, 316-10, 317-2, 317-5, 317-6, 317-7, 317-8, 317-9, 318-9, 318-10, 318-11, 319-1, 319-2, 319-4, 319-5, 319-6, 319-7, 319-8, 319-9, 319-10, 320-1, 320-2, 320-4, 320-5, 320-6, 320-7, 320-8

Photographs Max Leitner, Stuttgart: 44, 45

Bibliography: db Deutsche Bauzeitung 02/1992, TV Kohlensäure FFM, **Junge Beiträge zur Architektur,** Verlag H. M. Nelte, Wiesbaden 1993, ISBN 9783980346603, **Wettbewerbe Aktuell** 11/1994, S-Bahn Filderstadt, **Architekten in Baden Württemberg 1**, Verlag Buch und Film, Niedernhausen 1998, ISBN 9783933687005, **BM Möbel – Innenausbau** 09/1999, Penthouse Sauter-Stodal, **Architekturführer Tübingen,** Architektenkammer Baden-Württemberg, 2002, ISBN 3000101713, **Architekten in Baden Württemberg 2**, Verlag Buch und Film, Niedernhausen 2002, ISBN 9783933687098, **HÄUSER** 06/2002, portfolio, **Architekten in Deutschland,** Verlag Buch und Film, Niedernhausen 2003, ISBN 9783933687111, **proarchitectura** 03/2004, Miki 1, **Casa D** No. 12, 07–08/2004, Miki 1, **40 Rooms**, avedition, Ludwigsburg 2004, ISBN 9783899860160, **Der optimale Grundriss**, DVA, München 2004, ISBN 9783421034694, **Architekturstadtplan Stuttgart,** Verlagshaus Braun, Berlin 2005, ISBN 9783935455794, **BDA Baden-Württemberg – Ausgezeichnete Häuser,** avedition, Ludwigsburg 2006, ISBN 9783899860801, **HÄUSER** 02/2006, Miki 1, **BDA Architektur in Baden-Württemberg,** Karl Krämer Verlag, Stuttgart 2006, ISBN 9783782840439, **HÄUSER** 03/2006, Dornhalde, **Architekturführer Stuttgart,** Dietrich Reimer Verlag, Berlin 2006, ISBN 9783496012900, **Architekten in Baden Württemberg 3,** Verlag Buch und Film, Niedernhausen 2006, ISBN 9783933687159, **Architektur neues Stuttgart,** Verlagshaus Braun, Berlin 2006, ISBN 9783935455893, **1000 x European Architecture**, Verlagshaus Braun, Berlin 2007, ISBN 9783938780107, **HÄUSER** 05/2007, B-Wald, cover story, **Best of Häuser**, Callwey, München 2007, ISBN 9783766717184, **dds, Magazin für Möbel und Ausbau** 11/2007, Dornhalde, **Bauen für Zwei,** DVA, München 2008, ISBN 9783421035691, **HÄUSER special** 03/2008, Die 100 besten Einfamilienhaus-Architekten in Deutschland, Österreich und der Schweiz, Miki 1, Robo, **Home! Best of living design,** Verlagshaus Braun, Berlin 2008, ISBN 9783938780541, **AIT** 07–08/2008, Am Oberen Berg, **H.O.M.E.** 07/2008, Exhibition Houses, Art gallery, **idfx** 09/2008, B-Wald, **Die neue Villa,** Callwey, München 2008, ISBN 9783766717665, **Luxury Houses – Top of the world,** teNeues, Kempen 2008, ISBN 9783832792398, **Mies van der Rohe Award 2009** 12/2008, Nominated works for the European Union Prize for contemporary architecture, **Aktuelle Architektur in Stuttgart**, 26 Beispiele hervorragender Gegenwartsarchitektur in Stuttgart, Architektenkammer Baden-Württemberg, 2009, **md** 01/2009, Heidehof, **discret** 01/2009, Conte, **H.O.M.E.** 02/2009, Am Oberen Berg, homestory, **Architektur & Wohnen** 01/2009, Deutschlands 50 beste Einfamilienhäuser, Dornhalde, **Drink! Best of Bar Design,** Verlagshaus Braun, Berlin 2009, ISBN 9783037680155, **H.O.M.E.** 06–07/2009, Strauss, **Arquitectura & Construção** 06–07/2009, Heidehof, **Ecological Living,** teNeues, Kempen 2009, ISBN 9783832793067, **HÄUSER** 05/2009, Heidehof, **d2 Buenos Aires** 10/2009, Am Oberen Berg, **Neue Architektur Stuttgart,** Junius Verlag, Berlin 2009, ISBN 9783885064541, **Haus & Wellness** 10–11/2009, Heidehof, **Genuss & Feinsinn** autumn 2009, Alexander Brenner, **Haus & Wellness** 01/2010, Am Oberen Berg, cover story, **made** 01–02/2010 cover story, **Living & Design** No. 18, April 2010, Am Oberen Berg, **CONDE** No. 214, September 2010, Heidehof, **Living & Design** No. 24, October 2010, Heidehof, **Hausträume** 02/2011, Am Oberen Berg, **Kurier** 07/2011, Interview Alexander Brenner, **Kulturkalender** 07–08/2011, Alexander Brenner, **HÄUSER** 05/2011, Energie Special – Haus Strauss, **Häuser des Jahres,** Callwey, München 2011, ISBN 9783766719010, **Alexander Brenner – Houses**, Callwey, München 2011, ISBN 9783766718884, **Private Art Collections BW**, Fenkart-Njie, Stuttgart 2011, ISBN 9783000358357, **Moj Dom** 10/2011, B-Wald, **1.000 x European Architecture**, Braun Publishing, Salenstein 2011, ISBN 9783037680872, **Archipendium 2012,** archimappublishers, Berlin 2011, ISBN 9783940874337, **Wohn!Design** 01–02/2012, Architekturportrait Alexander Brenner, **Das Dicke Deutsche Hausbuch** 01/2012, Am Oberen Berg, **Inspiration Design** 01/2012, Am Oberen Berg, Heidehof, Interview, **Home Sweet Home – Ausgezeichnete Häuser,** BDA Stuttgart, 2012, **Wallpaper** 04/2012, Strauss, **Mein schönes Zuhause** 06–07/2012, Am Oberen Berg, **AIT** 07–08/2012, Alexander Brenner, **Luxuswohnen** 02/2012, Heidehof, **Auto Motor und Sport** 27/2012, SU House, **Archipendium 2013,** archimappublishers, Berlin 2012, ISBN 9783940874443, **Baumeister** 02/2013, Portrait Alexander Brenner, **Artravel** 49/2013, SU House, **home! – Best of Living Design,** Braun Publishing, Salenstein 2013, ISBN 9783037681299, **Casa Vogue** 03/2013, SU House, **H.O.M.E.** 03/2013, Vista House, **Attitude** 03–04/2013, SU House, **Casa Galeria – Luxury Living** 04–05/2013, SU House, **Cube** 06/2013, Am Oberen Berg, **Karl** 01/2013, SU, House, Vista House, Strauss, **Atrium** 05/2013, SU House, **CasaViva** 05/2013, Vista House, **Masterpieces: Bungalow Architecture + Design,** Braun Publishing, Salenstein 2013 ISBN 9783037681459, **AIT** 07–08/2013, SU House, **HÄUSER** 05/2013, SU House, **Haus & Auto – internationale Projekte,** Callwey, München 2013, ISBN 9783766720399, **AD – Best of Germany** 10/2013, SU House, **TOP Magazin** 10/2013, Interview Alexander Brenner, **Stuttgart – Architektur des 20. und, 21. Jahrhunderts**, Verlag Braun, Karlsruhe 2013, ISBN 9783765086120, **Designing Ways** 05/2013, SU House, **PUR: Minimalistische Wohnhäuser heute,** DVA, München 2013, ISBN 9783421038197, **CasaViva** 10/2013, SU House, **Villas: Superb Residential Style,** Braun Publishing, Salenstein 2013 ISBN 9783037681589, **Archipendium 2014,** archimappublishers, Berlin 2014, ISBN 9783940874733, **Luxury Home Design** 05/2013, SU House, **Spa & Home** März/April 2014, SU House, **bauhandwerk** 03/2014, Vista House, **77 Treppen für Wohnhäuser,** DVA, München 2014, ISBN 9783421039552, **DETAIL** 03/2014, Vista House, **Schwimmbad & Sauna** 05–06/2014, Vista House, **TREND** 49/2014, SU House, **Spa & Home** März/April 2014, SU House, **casamia** 02/2014, Robo, **Atrium – Spezial – Bäder** 06/2014, SU House, **ConstruARCH** 05–06/2014, SU House, **Prestige Design** Nr. 04/2014, SU House, **Die Villa heute – Baukultur und Lebensart,** DVA, München 2014, ISBN 9783421039507, **Neue Bungalows und Atriumhäuser,** DVA, München 2014, ISBN 9783421039071, **Vorbildliche Grundrisse,** DVA, München 2014, ISBN 9783421039583, **Living in Style,** Braun Publishing, Salenstein 2014, ISBN 9783037681770, **HÄUSER** 06/2014, An der Achalm, **Moderne Gartenkonzepte,** Becker Joest Volk Verlag, Hilden 2015, ISBN 9783954530700, **Habitare** Ano 12 No. 51, SU House, **Häuser am Hang,** DVA, München 2015, ISBN 9783421040053, **Atlas of European Architecture,** Braun Publishing, Salenstein 2015, ISBN 9783037681923, **Häuser des Jahres,** Callwey, München 2015, ISBN 9783766721662, **Concrete – Pure.Strong.Surprising,** Braun Publishing, Salenstein 2015, ISBN 9783037681893, **Das ideale Heim** Mai 2015, SU House, **AIT** 7-8.2015 SOL House, **md** 5.2015 Alexander Brenner, Haptik Event, **European House**, Images Publishing Group 2015, ISBN 9781864706369, **AIT** 10.2015 Exhibition Alexander Brenner, **100 Deutsche Häuser** 2015/2016, SU House, **inspiration Design!** 1.2016, SU House, **Neues Wohnen zwischen Drinnen und Draussen**, DVA, München 2016, ISBN 9783421039606, **AIT** 3.2016, Alexander Brenner – Villas and Houses 2010-2015, **Best of HÄUSER - Grandios gebaut,** Sonderheft 2016, An der Achalm, **55 Traumhäuser**, DVA, München 2016, ISBN 9783421040404, **HÄUSER** 6.2016, Bredeney House, **inspiration design!** 1.2017, Haus Miki 1, **Stilpunkte** 1.2017, Haus am Oberen Berg , **inspiration architektur!** 1.2017, Vista House, **CUBE** 2.2017, Bredeney House, **Living in Wood**, Braun Publishing, Salenstein 2017, ISBN 9783037682180, **Elle Decoration** 4.2017, SU House, **The Plan** #101 10.2017, Bredeney House, **CUBE** 12.2017, House an der Achalm, **Architekturführer Stuttgart**, DOM Publishers, Berlin 2018, ISBN 9783869224688, **HÄUSER** 6.2018, Haus am Wald, **Edle Einbaumöbel**, DVA, München 2018, ISBN 9783421040688, **COVETED EDITION** 12.2018, SU House, **Minimalist and Luxury Living Spaces**, Images Publishing Group 2018, ISBN 9781864708011, **smartLiving** März 2019, Haus Rudolph, **Atrium** 3.2019, Rottmann House, **My private Spa**, Braun Publishing, Salenstein 2019, ISBN 9783037682456, **smartLiving** November 2019, SU House, **HÄUSER** 6.2019, Brenner Research House PR39, **AIT** 3.2020, Brenner Research House PR39, **Villa Design**, Braun Publishing, Salenstein 2020, ISBN 9783037682630, **md** 4.2020, Brenner Research House PR39, **CUBE** 2.2020, Brenner Research House PR39, **Fascination Concrete**, Braun Publishing, Salenstein 2020, ISBN 9783037682647, **CUBE s**elect 3.2020, Interview Alexander Brenner, Brenner Research House PR39, **ATRIUM** 5.2020, Brenner Research House PR39, **interior fashion** 6.2020, Brenner Research House PR39, **opus C** Dezember 2020, Brenner Research House PR39, **Optamag** 01.2021, Brenner Research House PR39, **haus+wellness** April 2021, Vista House, **Hortus Conclusus**, Braun Publishing, Salenstein 2021, ISBN 9783037682692, **The Frankfurter** 3.2021, Brenner Research House PR39, **Bungalow Design**, Braun Publishing, Salenstein 2021, ISBN 9783037682739, **Villa Magazine** No.12, Fineway House, Heidehof, **CUBE select** 3.2022, Interview Alexander Brenner, **HÄUSER** 3.2022, Rudolph House, **CUBE** 4.2022, Rudolph House, **Architektur, Atmosphäre, Wahrnehmung - Die römische Villa als Chance für das Bauen heute**, Springer VS, Wiesbaden, 2022, ISBN 9783658223212, **ATRIUM** 5.2022, Fineway House

Viele liebe Menschen haben zu den Werken und zu den Abbildungen im Buch beigetragen. Allen Beteiligten ein ganz großes Dankeschön! Wie auch bei den vorhergehenden zwei Bänden haben diese beiden Engelchen das Material gesichtet, ausgewählt, gefügt und es neben den täglichen Aufgaben in altbewährter Teamarbeit in Form gebracht. Trotz der Mühen hatten wir großen Spaß daran, es entstehen zu sehen. Marc Büchler gilt mein allergrößter Dank. Wir hoffen beide, dass die Leidenschaft, die wir hineingegeben haben, ein wenig herausgelesen werden kann.

Many dear people have contributed to the projects and to the illustrations in this book. A huge thank you to everyone involved! As with the previous two volumes, these two little angels sifted through and selected the material, put it together and, in addition to their daily tasks, gave it shape in time-tested teamwork. Despite the effort, we had great fun watching the book evolve. I owe my deepest gratitude to Marc Büchler. We both hope that the passion we put into this volume is tangible.